How to survive middle age

Also by Christopher Matthew

A Different World: Stories of Great Hotels
Diary of a Somebody
The Long-Haired Boy
Loosely Engaged
The Crisp Report
Three Men in a Boat (annotated edition with Benny Green)

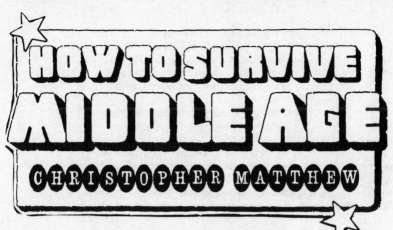

HOW TO SURVIVE MIDDLE AGE

CHRISTOPHER MATTHEW

PAVILION
MICHAEL JOSEPH

First published in Great Britain in 1983 by
Pavilion Books Limited
196 Shaftesbury Avenue, London WC2H 8JL
in association with Michael Joseph Limited
44 Bedford Square, London WC1B 3DU

Designed by Lawrence Edwards
Photoset by Rowland Phototypesetting Limited
Bury St Edmunds, Suffolk
Printed and bound by Billings and Sons Ltd, Worcester

British Library Cataloguing in Publication Data
Matthew, Christopher
How to survive middle age.
1. Middle age – Anecdotes, facetial, satire etc
I. Title
305.2'44'0207   HQ1061

ISBN 0-907516-18-1

Contents

To James Taylor
who is definitely
more middle-aged than me

I am enormously indebted to all those friends and experts whose ears I have bent on the subject of middle age and who have entered so splendidly into the spirit of the exercise – in particular, Geoffrey Aquilina-Ross, Adrian and Fiona Bailey, Peter Ballard, Christopher Branch, Dr Rob Buckman, Ricci Burns, Nicholas Coleridge, Lawrence Edwards, Mark Gilbert, Valerie Gilbert, David Hamilton of Wig Specialities Limited, Sandy Hamilton, Robin Kirk (Principal of Inglewood Health Hydro), Mr Leigh of Harrods' Men's Hairdressing Department, Michael and Michele Macdonald, A. V. Masters, M.I.T., Dr Magnus Pyke, Des and Claire Rayner, Tim Rice, C. Graham Smith of Westside Health Club, Peter Tickner of Richards Longstaff Limited, Daniel Topolski, and Patricia White.

Special thanks are also due to a number of people without whose help and encouragement the book would never have been finished in time, or indeed started – to my publisher Colin Webb whose idea it was in the first place and whose unfailing enthusiasm for the project has cheered me on whenever I have showed signs of flagging in my task; to Stephen and Dawn Oliver whose generosity in lending me their spare room and forbearance at my constant to-ings and fro-ings, usually during mealtimes, enabled me to clock up a thousand words a day *and* enjoy my summer holiday in Aldeburgh; to Judy Dauncey who, in addition to her usual painstaking editorial skills, joined forces with Claire Ternan to retype a largely illegible manuscript in a miraculously short space of time; and most of all to my wife Wendy for putting up yet again with all the gloom, anxiety and general rattiness that seems to attend the production of every new Matthew *oeuvre*.

Introduction

I had better begin straightaway by declaring an interest in this book. I am a middle-aged man.

Let me rephrase that. I am over forty. Forty-three to be exact, at the time of writing. And a bit.

Good gracious, I hear you exclaim. Forty-three? You call that middle-aged? A man in the prime of life, at the height of his mental powers? A man of fifty-three might justifiably describe himself as middle-aged, getting on, of advancing years, whatever way you care to put it; but at *forty-three*! A mere stripling.

Well now, funnily enough, those are very much the sort of lines along which I have been thinking myself.

All right, so let us say the average chap is seventy when he is finally cut down like the withered grass or however it is the psalm has it. In which case, if one wishes to be really pedantic about these things, I passed the middle-age mark eight years ago and from now on it is, as a twenty-one-year-old friend of mine was once informed by his tutor as he took his leave at the end of his final term at Oxford, a straight run to the grave.

Fortunately, however, or unfortunately, depending how you view these things, life is not like one of those wonderful journeys by Swiss Railways on which you can be absolutely certain that if you set out on the 10.46 from Geneva you will be at Lausanne at precisely 11.25, Vevey at 11.41 and at Aigle exactly seventeen minutes later.

If anything, it is more like a journey on British Rail which, given

7

that it begins on time, or indeed at all, is pretty well guaranteed, thanks to various hitches along the way ranging from the technical (ice on the points at Didcot) to the human (a sudden work-to-rule by the local branch of the footplatemen's union at Rugby), to ensure that not only will one miss every connection along the line, but that whoever is coming to meet one at the other end is in for a long, boring wait on a draughty platform with a closed refreshment room and very probably a parking ticket. Naturally no satisfactory explanations will be forthcoming. Actually, the one similarity between a journey on BR and life is that in both cases only God knows exactly what time one's due in. For the rest of us humble travellers, it's anybody's guess.

The fact is that in this day of medical miracles, when more and more of us are managing not only to stagger further and further into our ninth and even tenth decades but actually feel quite perky for it, middle age is fast becoming something of a movable feast, recognisable less by any definite date than by a series of symptoms – some obvious, some indefinable – reminding us that we are, as the euphemism goes, not as young as we used to be. These can range from the purely physical (not being able to stay out after midnight) to the mental (walking into a room to get something and standing there, wondering what it could possibly be) to the philosophical (is there life after death and, if so, do I still keep my old VAT registration number?)

All sorts of wits have come up with sharp aphorisms intended to encapsulate the sensations of approaching middle age. You know the sort of thing:

Middle age occurs when you are too young to take up golf and too old to rush up to the net. *Franklin Pierce Adams*

Middle age is the time when a man is always thinking that in a week or two he will feel as good as ever. *Don Marquis*

You will recognise, my boy, the first sign of age; it is when you go out into the streets of London and realise for the first time how young the policemen look. *Seymour Hicks*

There are three ways to tell if you're getting on: people of your own age start looking older than you; you become convinced you're suddenly equipped with a snooze button;

and you start getting symptoms in the places you used to get urges. *Denis Norden*

I always thought you'd reached middle age when you started growing hair inside your ears. *My dentist.* (See also section on Teeth)

Others have expressed their feelings about middle age in *aperçus* which, while being equally mordant, have an added sense of sadness and self-pity.

When, in Arthur Pinero's play *The Second Mrs Tanqueray*, the middle-aged bachelor Cayley Drummle tells the daughter of his old friend Aubrey Tanqueray that he saw her out walking and she replies that she did not see him, he comments wistfully, 'It is my experience, my dear, that no charming young lady of nineteen ever does see a man of forty-five.' A case of fishing for compliments if ever I heard one.

Frankly, were I ever moved to crack witty on the subject (and who is to say that by the end of this book I shall not have achieved my ambition to make it into the *Penguin Dictionary of Modern Quotations?*) I'd go for the more positive line, like Pope John XXIII who is reputed to have said (to a fellow cardinal perhaps who was losing his confidence), 'Men are like wine. Some turn to vinegar, but the best improve with age.' Or like Henry David Thoreau, always a man with a saw or two up his sleeve (no joke intended), who characteristically viewed the whole process of ageing in terms of woodwork. 'The youth,' he wrote, 'gets together materials for a bridge to the moon, and at length the middle-aged man decides to make a woodshed of them.'

While there is a lot to be said for settling at a certain age for what one is, one finds it hard not to sympathise to some extent with the greying advertising copywriter who continues to plug away into the small hours convinced that he is the, as yet undiscovered, natural successor to T. S. Eliot.

For my own part, I am quite unable to view my present way of life as anything other than a fluke, so little relation does it appear to bear to anything that has gone before.

At school I showed not the slightest talent for, or interest, in anything other than getting by with the least personal hardship. In this I was moderately successful. At university I unearthed a hitherto dormant passion for performing on the stage, largely in slightly sub-standard revue work of the sort that people of my parents' generation tend to refer to as 'showing off'. Rarely did I set pen to paper other than to accept invitations to weekends in the country. As for my undistinguished five-year stint among the fleshpots of various London advertising agencies in the sixties, I am still at a complete loss to explain how this could possibly have developed in any logical way out of a brief, if eventful, career in Switzerland as an assistant master in a girls' finishing school, teaching English and General Behaviour.

At the age of forty I was living, as I had been for many years, in a small bachelor flat near Battersea Park, happily unencumbered by wives, children, mortgage, school fees and life insurance premiums. I saw myself sliding gently into middle age with my books, my thick woollen dressing gown, my small but reliable repertoire of Norwegian Provincial/South London/Middle Indian dishes and my slightly larger, though equally dependable, circle of friends and acquaintances – most of them married, most of them only too happy to ring me up at the last minute and invite me to contribute my wit and youthful *joie de vivre* to their dinner tables.

And yet, blow me down, here I am, less than three years later, a paterfamilias figure, complete with wife, small children, dog, house in south London, insurances, mortgages, debts, acting the part of an eager twenty-five-year-old despite the evidence that stares out at me from the bathroom mirror every morning – the lines, the jowls, the grey hairs, the fistfuls of flesh where the waist used to be, the unmistakable look of a man who knows that the race against time is on in earnest and he's twenty years behind at the starting line.

If I must believe, when I first set out to make my fame and fortune twenty years ago, that I thought radically differently about such fundamental matters as food, drink, love, sex, Tony Benn etc., then I suppose I must. But if I am being really truthful, I have to say that my mental processes appear to me to be in as good a nick as ever they were – if not marginally better.

It is this total failure of mind and body to keep pace one with the other that all too often transforms a man's middle years (say forty to sixty for the sake of simplification) from a period of contentment and mellow fruitfulness to one of anger, frustration, pain and more or less constant humiliation.

And since I am on the subject and have succeeded in working myself into something of a state about it, I hope you will not mind too much if I get the whole thing off my chest once and for all. The point is this.

The human race has a great deal to put up with at the hands of 'Dame' Nature. Indeed, it would appear that she enjoys nothing better than seeing us writhing in shame and agony as a result of yet another of her practical jokes. The crueller the trick, the happier she is.

This can range from the irritating (the angry spot that comes up on the side of one's nose minutes before one is about to venture out on a first dinner date) to the genuinely damaging (the actor who lands his first romantic part only to develop, for no reason at all, advanced halitosis). None of us knows for certain when the metaphorical knee may not be *en route* towards the groin or whether the proffered hand is not about to catch us a sharp one round the side of the head. But of all the beastly, underhand tricks Nature has up her sleeve, none is beastlier or more underhand than allowing the mind to remain as young and lively and eager for life as ever it was, while the body slowly disintegrates around it.

It isn't so much the fact of this tragic discrepancy that distresses and humiliates as the appalling manner in which it is borne upon us.

One might, after all, be forgiven for supposing that the Almighty in His infinite wisdom and kindness would have had the common decency, and foresight, to equip us with some in-built device designed to warn us that we are fast approaching a stage in our lives when we are no longer quite as young as we like to think we are. Not only would this help to adapt to the onset of middle age by reminding us that the time had come to get our hair cut, give up body-hugging shirts and generally stop trying to impress young girls, but more importantly it would save us all such a fearful amount of unnecessary embarrassment and money.

A woman friend of mine to this day blushes to the roots of her hair at the memory of an incident at a party given by some friends of hers for their daughters who were all of ten years her junior. She freely admits to never having been the most loose-limbed and imaginative of dancers, but, not wishing to appear a fuddy-duddy, she had taken to the floor of the little discotheque that had been rigged up in the cellar. She was prancing about innocently enough with the father of the house and had even begun to acquire sufficient confidence to try a modest improvisation or two when she overheard a young girl commenting to her partner, 'How pathetic it is to see the middle-aged making such fools of themselves.'

If they think that's pathetic, they want to see us trying to get the children up and off to school in the mornings, or stumbling about in the parents' Egg and Spoon, or trying to explain The Twist to an eighteen-year-old, or lying awake at night worrying about whether to go for the Whole Life Assurance with Profits or settle for the Increasable and Renewable Term Assurance. Or indeed anything.

The trouble with middle age is that one can't win. On the one hand one is mentally more agile than ever, but one knows too much about the pitfalls of life to be able to plump confidently for what one knows in one's water to be the right course. Everyone around us who depends upon us assumes that we must be capable of making all the right decisions, and so, on the face of it, we should. But there are so many qualifying factors to be considered in even the simplest situation that, before we know what, we have settled for a stupid compromise that satisfies no one – least of all ourselves.

We have no excuses to offer as we did when we were young ('silly young fool'), or will when we are old ('silly old fool'), and no one is going to show us the slightest sympathy if we get things wrong.

Nine times out of ten we have no financial training or experience whatsoever, yet we must pick our way through the small print in dozens of life policies and from the murky depths of verbiage pull out a nugget of pure gold.

Our knowledge of modern educational methods is often extremely sketchy, yet we must decide whether to devote such little as is left over from our income after the building society, the office pension scheme and the local supermarket have taken their cut, to treating our offspring to a private education or tossing them with a shrug of the shoulders into the circus ring of the comprehensive system.

We barely comprehend the workings of the push-bike, yet we must balance the various advantages of the Datsun Cherry, the Ford Fiesta, the Daihatsu Charade and the Vauxhall Chevette, and come home at the end of the day with something that will take a family of four comfortably to the West Country complete with luggage, self-catering equipment, booze for a fortnight, dog and windsurfer, at an average speed of 60 mph and an average fuel consumption rate of 37 mpg, *and* has a cigarette lighter and all the other luxury items which on similar vehicles come as extras, *and* will stop on a sixpence, *and* comes with a year's free breakdown insurance (parts *and* labour), *and* in a colour that doesn't have the wife wincing visibly every time she opens the garage door. Dante of course hit the nail on the head as usual in the opening lines of the *Divine Comedy*:

> Midway this way of life we're bound upon,
> I woke to find myself in a dark wood,
> Where the right road was wholly lost and gone.

I know just how he felt. Mark you, if that was the way life was getting to him in the fourteenth century, I dread to think how he'd have coped during an ASLEF strike in the 1980s.

A chap called Wallis in a book called *The Challenge of Middle Age*, which I came upon recently in my local library, goes even further and suggests that middle age is really just like adolescence all over again.

His theory, for what it is worth, is that the menopause, with all its biological changes, parallels the dawn of sexuality in puberty – viz: changes in appearance, a sudden increase in bodily weight, an urgent need to conceal physical changes, clumsiness, depression, 'an upsurge of erotic social-sexual behaviour', an overwhelming urge to safeguard oneself against authority, plus a general lack of sympathy all round from friends and family alike.

He may have a point.

Oddly enough, I have felt the odd spot coming up in recent months – something I have not experienced since schooldays, and had rather proudly ascribed it to a healthy case of rising sap. My social-sexual behaviour on the other hand appears to have been no more and no less erotic than usual, but, should my luck suddenly change and I find it impossible to keep my hands off women's buttocks at cocktail parties, I shall certainly know what to put it down to, even if the women in question do not quite see it the same way. I can only hope Mr Wallis will be prepared to back his theories with hard words by turning up and giving evidence on my behalf in court.

At the same time, I see no reason to use my age as an excuse for outrageous behaviour. I have never felt myself inordinately drawn towards young girls or older women nor, as far as I am aware, have they to me. I can predict with some degree of confidence, therefore, that whatever other nonsense my hormonal balances may get me up to in the years ahead, the nation's womanhood can sleep easy in their beds at night.

Or can I?

I am already beginning to display the oddest symptoms which I certainly cannot recollect noticing in my younger days. I noticed recently, for instance, that when weeding the herbaceous border, I have taken to emitting small but distinct grunts every time I bend forward. It's all right when I'm kneeling – except, that is, for the twinge in the capella which I put down to an old skiing injury; but it's when I'm *standing* and bending that I get this grunting business. I'm wondering if it's psychological, and if so, what other uncharacteristic and unattractive behaviour might I not find myself displaying without realising it? Time will doubtless tell – and so, presumably, will my wife.

Whatever else people may say about middle age (and a lot of people say a lot of things about middle age), the only sure thing about it is that, whether it hits us sooner or later, whether it creeps up on us slowly like dry rot or sloshes us between the eyes like a wild tee shot, whether we are prepared to admit that it has arrived or choose to put it down to feeling slightly unfit and under the weather, for those of us who are privileged to live that long, it is an inescapable fact of life. Given its inevitable existence, the problem then is (a) how to recognise it when it does strike, (b) how to cope with the shock of realisation that one is middle-aged and (c) how to get through it and into old age with as much courage and dignity and enjoyment as is humanly possible.

Which is what this book is all about.

Incidentally, I apologise in advance to all those middle-aged ladies who were hoping I might come up with an answer or two to their worries. Unfortunately, this would require a quite separate book, possibly several. For the moment, I've got enough problems of my own.

I should also like to point out that several of the cross-references in this book are untraceable. At the time, I had every intention of following all of them up. However, the one thing you learn when you get to my age is that life is full of little disappointments, and these, I'm afraid, are just a few more of them.

In which I call upon Dr Magnus Pyke, who
describes what actually happens in middle
age to various parts of our bodies – skin,
bones, eyes, brain, taste, balance etc., and
set a simple test to determine whether the
reader is middle-aged and, if so, *how*
middle-aged.

Chapter One

Before we crack on with an outline of some of the main problems posed by the onset of middle age, with suggestions as to possible ways of combating them, I think it would be helpful if we were to look at the subject, first of all, from the purely medical and physiological point of view.

Much serious scientific work has been done on the subject of ageing in recent years (the names of Lansing, Stoehler and Korenschevsky spring immediately to mind), and I doubt that any observations I may have to make upon the subject will add significantly to, say, Lansing, Rosenthal and Kamen's 'Effect of age on calcium binding in mouse liver' (1949), or even Laws and Purves's 'The earplug of the *Mysticeti* as an indication of age, with special reference to the North Atlantic Fin Whale' (1956).

However, new knowledge can often spring from the most unexpected sources. I do not pretend to be a scientist, but if, in the years to come, some little nugget of mine should ever prove to be of use to science and my humble researches find their way into the bibliographical list at the back of some learned tome, I cannot say I shall be all that surprised.

At all events, one does one's best and that includes, of course, picking the brains of the best experts available.

You will understand, therefore, the depth of my disappointment when my publishers turned down my suggestion (on the grounds of cost, as usual) that they fly me out to California for a serious session with one of the world's foremost experts on the process of ageing, Dr Alex Comfort.

His book *Ageing: The Biology of Senescence* (1954) is a masterpiece of scientific research. I must confess that certain sections worry me, viz: his 'Survival Curve on the Orkney Vole'.

I also have my reservations re his inclusion of Gompertz's attempt to depict the age-decline in terms of actuarial mathematics expressed in the function:

$$R_m = -\frac{1}{n} \times \frac{dn}{dt} = R_o e \propto t$$

On the other hand, his conclusion is thoroughly sound. 'Senescence,' he writes, 'like Mount Everest, challenges our ingenuity by the fact that it is there, and the focussing of our attention on it is unlikely to be fruitless.'

I could not agree more.

Anyway, while waiting for the great man to pay one of his rare visits to our shores, I thought I should fill in the time with some background reading based on his excellent bibliography.

Picking four works at random – Abdel-Malek's 'Susceptibility of the snail *Biomphalaria boissyi* to infection with certain strains of *Schistosoma mansoni*'; Brown, Sinclair, Cronk and Clark's 'Some remarks on premature ageing in the Eskimos'; Fitch's 'Early sexual maturity and longevity under natural conditions in the Great Plains narrow-mouthed frog'; and, perhaps most germane of all, Blunck's 'Lebensdauer, Fortpflanzungsvermögen und Alterserscheinungen beim Geilbrand' – I headed eagerly for my local library, only to return a very, very disappointed man. However, a chance conversation with Dr Rob Buckman reminded me that no serious study of middle age should be attempted without reference to Dr Magnus Pyke's book *Long Life: Expectations for Old Age* and, if possible, a chat with the great man himself.

I was slightly surprised that my name did not mean more to the doctor when I phoned, and he appeared curiously vague about my work. However, when two communicators get together, reputation is of little consequence and within minutes of my arrival at his house in Hammersmith we were swapping ideas as if we'd known each other for years.

Now I don't want to bore you with a lot of technical jargon at this point, so let me quickly provide you with a check-list, as outlined to me by Dr Pyke, of things in your body that individually start to pack up with the advancing years and which, when taken together, produce the effect known as middle age.

1. Calcium loss. As a child, one takes in calcium at such a rate that the entire calcium content of the skeleton is replaced every two years. However, the older one gets, the less one absorbs, until by the age of about forty-five one not only stops absorbing it, despite huge intakes of Vitamin D, but one actually starts losing the stuff.

This was sobering news. I cannot pretend that I have ever harboured ambitions to be the Heavyweight Boxing Champion of the World, nor do I have plans for taking up ice hockey next winter. However, the knowledge that my increasingly brittle frame has effectively put both pursuits well out of court is no less upsetting for that.

I'm seriously beginning to wonder if the increasing possibility of broken limbs might very soon put a stop to my motorcycling exploits. My 50 cc Honda engine may not be the most tigerish on the market, but only the other day I was kick-starting it and barked my shin quite badly, leaving a nasty bruise. It only goes to show.

2. It seems that my physical strength is draining away by the minute. According to an article in the January 1962 edition of *Scientific American* by one Nathan W. Shock (no comment), the power of a hand-grip of a man of seventy-five is a mere 55 per cent of that of a thirty-year-old which can't be good news for elderly masons.

However, this fact is unlikely to give me sleepless nights since (a) there appears to be no scientific evidence to prove that the power exerted by the fingers on a pen directly affects the quality, style or selling potential of the written word upon which I depend for my livelihood, and (b), as Dr Pyke points out in his book, 'Experience in shipwrecks . . . has often shown that it is less muscular castaways who survive when their more powerful companions lose hope.' In the light of this fascinating news, I am seriously reconsidering the possibility of a long sea cruise next winter.

3. Water. The older we become, the more blunted becomes our sense of thirst, as a result of which we can easily become dehydrated without realising it. This may well account for my increasing fondness for a large whisky and soda or two of an early

evening. Nature is a wonderful compensator, I've often heard it said.

4. The brain. Like any other muscle, this decreases with age. I am certainly not aware of my own grey matter being at its bulkiest at the age of twenty-five, as Dr Pyke would have us believe. Indeed, in many ways I was a peculiarly dim young man. Nor, if what the doctor tells me is true, can I honestly get myself terribly worked up about it one way or the other.

Given that my brain is at present about the size of a grapefruit, Winston Churchill's must have been nearer that of a moderately sized Jaffa orange when he took the reins of power in 1940. Yet he seemed none the worse for it. And there was old P. G. Wodehouse, bashing away at the typewriter at the age of ninety-three, driven by something little larger than a Cox's Orange Pippin.

5. The older one gets, apparently, the more one forgets to shiver. I do not understand this. I can only suppose that this is one particular middle-aged disability that I have, for some reason, been spared.

6. At around middle age, human beings find it increasingly difficult to stand. Indeed a ninety-year-old finds it about as difficult to remain steady on his pins as a child of two.

Oddly enough, I have noticed a slight shakiness in myself recently. This may be directly related to my increasing intake of whisky and soda, although in the absence of carefully controlled scientific tests, I am not prepared to state this as an empirical fact.

7. According to Dr Pyke, scientific tests show that, when we are young, we have approximately 245 taste buds on our tongues, but when we are old, the average falls to ninety. He says that this would explain why we look back on our mother's indifferent cooking with such enthusiasm and why it is the very young who make such a hoo-ha over such comparatively innocuous tastes as rhubarb and mutton fat.

In my humble opinion, you cannot beat a plate of stewed rhubarb, provided it is well cooked. My own mother's stewed rhubarb tastes every bit as good today as it did forty years ago, and I should be happy for Dr Pyke to put it to the test whenever and wherever he wishes. On television if need be. Re mutton fat: since my loathing of this is as great today as it was in 1943, if not greater, I feel I am hardly in a position to comment with any degree of impartiality.

8. Loosening skin. This is presumably to accommodate the gathering fat (see sections on Health Farms, Exercise and passim).

9. Deterioration of eyesight. This goes without saying (see sections on Eyesight and Picking up Younger Women in Night Clubs).

10. Ditto gradual loss of hearing – although in my experience this can vary considerably depending on how loudly someone is speaking at the time (see sections on Deaf-Aids and Pop Music etc.)

11. Sex. Now this is a tricky one. I do not wish to pre-empt the chapter later in the book that deals fully and comprehensively with this subject. Suffice at this stage to say that Dr Pyke's advice was 'Get your sex over before you're fifty.'

While, *en principe*, I do not find the prospect of middle-aged individuals hurling themselves at each other in wild geriatric abandon particularly attractive, I should not care to think that Dr Pyke's dictum might be adopted by local authorities, social workers, marriage guidance counsellors etc. as a hard and fast rule.

Having myself recently fathered two boys over the age of forty (I mean that I am over forty, not the boys), I am not planning to repeat the experience (see section on Vasectomy). And yet Dr Hewlett Johnson, the 'Red' Dean of Canterbury, was well over sixty when he sired two magnificent daughters, whose proud frames graced the cathedral precincts when I was a boy at The King's School in the fifties, and set many of us wondering whether the public-school system of segregation was all it was cracked up to be.

Moreover, I do not believe I am alone when I say that the cinema industry and the acting profession in general would be a sadder and less colourful place had it not been for the vigour displayed in his latter years by the late Charlie Chaplin.

At the same time, while I cannot rule out the possibility that at the age of, say, fifty-nine or sixty-three, a chance look exchanged over a late night cup of Bournvita or an affectionate squeeze of the hand in the darkness of the Academy Cinema may lead to heaven knows what expressions of unbridled how's-your-father, I feel I must applaud Dr Pyke's outspokenness when he writes, *à propos* things not going quite so well bed-wise as in the heady days of yesteryear: 'In married life when the "life force" has had its way and sex becomes less important, the partners do not suddenly become less happy or less useful members of society; and there is no reason why they should not remain as devoted to each other and as fulfilled in their marriage as ever they were.'

Elsewhere he writes, 'There is a lot to be said for being old.' He might have said the same thing about being middle-aged. I'm only sorry more people do not see it the same way. So, it would seem, does Dr Pyke.

'The physiological imperative,' he said as he guided me towards the front door, 'is inexorable. You are *not* as young as you feel. People convince themselves that they can rebut the ageing process, but you can't, you know. Whatever anyone may try to tell you otherwise.'

As I drove home along the Cromwell Road extension on my Honda, rather more cautiously than is my wont, something the good doctor had said earlier on kept running through my head like a refrain.

'There are those,' he said, 'who can run marathons, and those who can't.'

How right he is. Horses for courses has always been one of the principles upon which I have based my life and I have no reason to suppose that I have been that wide of the mark.

Almost everyone I have spoken to about this book has replied (with extraordinary smugness in most cases, considering), 'Ah yes. Well, of course, middle age is a state of mind.'

I realise this is a fashionable view but frankly I cannot altogether go along with it.

As I see it, middle age is far more often a matter of what life makes of you than what you make of life. The idea that be-slippered feet automatically denote a be-slippered mind is just another of those facile observations that quite simply flies in the face of the facts. And the facts are that some are born middle-aged, some seem destined never to reach it, and some miss it out altogether. Here are some examples.

Category A:
Among those who arrived in the world middle-aged are:

Auberon Waugh
Robert Robinson
Henry Cooper
Philip Larkin
Prince Charles
Richard Ingrams
Timothy West
Robin Day
Ray Illingworth
Matt Monro

Category B:
Men who seem destined never to reach middle age include:

Tony Benn
Cliff Richard
Melvyn Bragg
David Attenborough
David Bailey
Paul McCartney
André Previn
Alan Bennett (physically a schoolboy but mentally he belongs to Category A)
Dudley Moore
David Steel (see Alan Bennett)

Category C:
Those who appeared to move directly from extreme youth to extreme old age without passing through any intermediate stage:

John Betjeman
Malcolm Muggeridge
Michael Foot
Evelyn Waugh
W.H. Auden
Rex Harrison
Fred Astaire
Harold Macmillan

Prizes consisting of generous supplies of Grecian 2000, Philosan, Wincarnis and Valium will be awarded to readers who can add to this list in such a way that I and my publishers instantly kick ourselves and exclaim, 'How *could* we have forgotten him?' (Proof of purchase must be supplied with each entry.)

But this is all by way of fudging the issue. You know as well as I do whether or not you are middle-aged. If it had never so much as occurred to you that you might fit within that category, you would not have bought the book or been given it in the first place.

Therefore, the question you should be asking yourself at this stage is not whether or not you should take it back and exchange it for some entertaining volume on Ian Botham or the Princess of Wales's schooldays, but which sections are likely to be of most interest to you.

In other words, you have admitted to yourself that you are middle-aged, but *how* middle-aged? Are you right there, slap in the middle, or only on the fringes? Are you, to put it bluntly, barely middle-aged, slightly middle-aged, pretty well middle-aged, or completely and utterly middle-aged?

To help you decide, here is a simple test for you to do while sitting on the loo or in a deckchair or wherever it is you undertake such lighthearted *divertissements*.

1. Was Captain Carlson:
(a) A famous tennis star of the forties and fifties?
(b) The skipper of a ship that sank in dramatic circumstances in the Channel in the early fifties?
(c) The commander of a space vehicle in a popular boys' weekly in the fifties?
(d) A pop group in the early sixties?

2. Who was well-known for singing the praises of 'that humble, black-coated worker, the prune'?
(a) Lord Woolton, Minister of Food during the Second World War.
(b) Dr Charles Hill, the Radio Doctor of the forties and fifties.
(c) President Dwight D. Eisenhower.
(d) The President of the National Federation of Prune Producers of Southern California.

3. Who played Henry Bones, the younger member of the famous detective partnership of Norman and Henry Bones, the Boy Detectives, on *Children's Hour* in the forties and fifties?
(a) Denis Waterman, star of *The Sweeney* and *Minder*.
(b) Patricia Hayes, the distinguished actress.
(c) John Howard Davies, now head of BBC TV Comedy.
(d) Gerald Champion, who later gave it all up to become an executive in a soft drinks firm.

4. Was Skylon:
(a) A group of musicians who for a few memorable weeks in 1959 backed Cliff Richard?
(b) A feature of the Festival of Britain in 1951?
(c) An early type of ice lolly?
(d) A popular substance once used to dye trousers blue?

5. What was the name of the maid in the long-running BBC Radio series *Life with the Lyons*?
(a) Peggy
(b) Moggy.
(c) Maggie.
(d) Aggie.
And, for a bonus, name the two Lyon children.

6. Who in the early sixties referred to whom as 'a thoroughly filthy fellow'?
(a) Harold Macmillan to Mick Jagger.
(b) Harold Macmillan to Harold Wilson.
(c) Mervyn Griffith-Jones QC to D. H. Lawrence.
(d) Mervyn Griffith-Jones QC to Stephen Ward.

7. Was Harvey Orkin:
(a) An American spy-plane pilot?
(b) A wisecracking New York theatrical agent?
(c) An alias for Lee Harvey Oswald?
(d) The hero of some surrealistic film starring Anthony Newley?

8. If the monthly premium for a nine-year Term Assurance Life Policy is £7.60, with a death benefit of £20,000 with options to increase the benefit by 30 per cent after three and six years, but you choose instead to go for Whole Life Assurance with Profits (premiums payable through life) with a monthly premium of

£49.80, would the bonus added to the basic benefit in twenty-four years (assuming the current rate is maintained) be:
(a) £25,280?
(b) £38,860?
(c) £44,510?
(d) £49,520?

9. You are watching *News at Ten* when you are suddenly seized with a sharp pain in your left side. Do you:
(a) Assume you are suffering a coronary and call for an ambulance?
(b) Assume you are suffering from a bad go of indigestion and call for the Rennies?
(c) Assume you have been putting weight on again and loosen your waistcoat buttons?
(d) Assume it to be just another of those inexplicable aches and pains, pour yourself a reassuring whisky and soda, and spend the rest of the night awake panicking?

10. You feel it is high time you made a bit of an effort and took your seventeen-year-old and friend to the cinema. Do you:
(a) Take them to *Pink Floyd: The Wall*?
(b) Take them to a special showing at the NFT of *Les Enfants du Paradis*?
(c) Take them to the latest James Bond?
(d) Tell yourself you'll think about it and do nothing?

Answers to the middle-aged test
(Scoring out of 4)

1.(a) You are vaguely thinking of Colonel Teddy Tinling, the famous tennis-clothes designer, and possibly of a Swedish player called Lars something who was a regular at Wimbledon in the years immediately following the war. 2 points.
(b) Quite right. He was the captain of the *Flying Enterprise* which went down off the south coast in heavy seas in 1952 and made a name for himself by refusing to abandon ship until the last possible moment. 4 points.
(c) Shows a passing knowledge of the *Eagle* comic. 3 points.
(d) Anyone with the slightest knowledge of pop music in the

sixties knows that the days when whole groups went under the name of a single person or object were still a long way off. 1 point.

2.(a) Good effort. Displays knowledge of radio broadcasts by ministers during war years. 3 points.
(b) Correct. The Radio Doctor, later head of everything to do with television, was also famous for the observation that 'Another of Boxing Day's little troubles is constipation. Too much food and too much armchair and the body's reply is "What I have, I hold." ' 4 points.
(c) It's exactly the silly sort of thing American presidents used to come out with in the good old days before people started worrying about their images, and assassination by dried fruit became a very real possibility. So not such a silly answer. 2 points.
(d) A very silly answer and barely worth the 1 point.

3. (a) No, he played *Just William* on television as a boy, but warm. 3 points.
(b) Those for whom Miss Hayes' performances are an integral part of childhood can still scarcely believe that it is the same person who played *Edna, the Inebriate Woman*. 4 points.
(c) Shows you were of a cinema-going age in the forties when John, the Bonnie Langford of his day, was pulling them in up and down the country for his performances in *Oliver Twist, Tom Brown's Schooldays*, etc. But wrong. 2 points.
(d) A bit of a cheat this one. Gerald Campion played Billy Bunter on television in the fifties and Freddy Bartholomew, a well-known American child star of the thirties became a big cheese in a top advertising agency. However, for those with a fuddled memory, a consolatory 1 point, and an extra point for spotting the deliberate spelling mistake.

4. (a) Don't be daft. With the Shadows around?
(b) That and the Dome of Discovery were the two main reasons we were all so keen to go to the South Bank. Oh, and the Pleasure Gardens and Funfair in Battersea Park, of course. 4 very easy points.
(c) Perfectly feasible. 3 points.
(d) A variation of Dylon, no doubt? 2 points.

5. (a) No. 1 point.
(b) No. 2 points.

(c) Nearly. 3 points.
(d) Yes. 4 points.
Bonus question: Richard and Barbara. 5 points.

6. (a) Mr Macmillan's opinions of pop stars are not recorded. Suffice to say that it was his successor but one as PM, Mr Wilson, who was so keen to make up to the young voter that he arranged for the Beatles to have MBEs. 1 point.
(b) Far more likely. 2 points.
(c) Good thinking. Any man who cannot run to servants is bound to be a bit on the grubby side. 3 points.
(d) Any truly middle-aged man will know this as well as he knows the basic steps of The Twist. Mr Griffith Jones's remark, 'Is this the sort of man you would allow your servants to have their backs manipulated by?' is, however, thought to be apocryphal. Incidentally, I have always found the Profumo scandal an excellent means of assessing someone's age in case of doubt. A man of forty-three who finds himself spending a lot of time on a girl who thinks that Christine Keeler is an heiress to a large firm of marmalade manufacturers should start asking himself some serious questions. 4 points.

7. (a) I can't imagine who you're thinking of. 1 point.
(b) With Patrick Campbell on *TW3*, one of the great broadcasting stars of the early sixties. I miss him still. 4 points.
(c) For recognising a typical *Private Eye* misnomer. 2 points.
(d) For having heard of Anthony Newley. 3 points.

8. (a) You are obviously old enough that your maths have become decidedly rusty. 3 points.
(b) Only a truly middle-aged man would have agonised long and hard enough about life insurance to know what on earth the question means, let alone what the answer is. 4 points, plus a bonus of 5.
(c) Clearly a stab in the dark. 2 points.
(d) Only someone under the age of thirty-five could possibly hope for a figure approaching this. 1 point.

9. This is a trick question designed purely to encourage those younger readers who feel they are lagging behind. Since any of the answers could be counted acceptable behaviour for a middle-aged man, any one of them scores 4 points.

10. (a) Not really, unless you can't get into any of the other three films in the cinema complex. 1 point for desperation.
(b) Good thinking again. Old foreign films provide one with an excellent opportunity for boring the young about how they don't make panning shots/long dissolves/edits like that any more. 3 points.
(c) Ditto re early James Bond heroines – Shirley Eaton, Honor Blackman, Ursula Andress etc. 2 points.
(d) Any genuinely middle-aged man knows that if anything is any good, it will turn up sooner or later on television. Patience is a virtue. 4 points.

How You Scored

40 points and over: Congratulations. You are well and truly middle-aged, with an unhealthy penchant for nostalgia and a well-developed talent for boring the backsides off the young. This book was designed for people like you and you should waste no time whatsoever plunging ahead with Chapter 2. Possibly over a cup of Milo.
28-40 points: Good effort but you've still got a little way to go before you can really consider yourself to be of advancing years. The Beatles may be into their forties now, ditto the Stones, but there's a world of difference between those who screamed at their pop idols and those who thrilled silently to 'Ray's a Laugh' and 'Café Continental'. Certain chapters will nevertheless be right up your street, although I would venture to suggest you skip the sections on jogging, dogs, irrational fears and DIY.
15-27 points: A promising score on paper but I suspect that, you have garnered your knowledge from nostalgic TV programmes rather than from first-hand experience. On the other hand, no youngster who has sat through *Les Enfants du Paradis* can be all bad, and to you I say: Despair not; middle age is only just around the next bend.
Under 15 points: I don't suppose you'd even recognise a pair of slippers if they were served up to you on a plate, would you? Wrong subject, wrong book, wrong author.

In which I consider various well-tried
methods of combating the effects of the
advancing years – from hair transplants,
toupées, hair weaving, colourants and the
Robinson Sweep, to contact lenses, bifocals,
the harvesting of nasal hair, dentures, deaf
aids and cosmetic surgery.

Chapter Two

But enough of these delaying tactics and to our (slightly withered) onions.

Given that there is scarcely a square centimetre of our bodies that is not showing distinct signs of conking out from the age of forty onwards, what, if anything, is to be done about it?

Dr Pyke insists that it is impossible to rebut the ageing process, and I doubt there is a man alive who, unless he is a complete loony, does not in his heart of hearts know that he is quite right.

However, that is not to say that there are those who will not go to the most elaborate lengths imaginable to hold Father Time at bay until the last possible minute. Poor old Somerset Maugham for one.

Basically the rejuvenation business is divided sharply into two distinct schools of thought: the lifting school and the pumping school. Maugham favoured the latter.

Someone (possibly the Duke of Windsor) told him that there was a chap in Switzerland called Paul Niehans who could work wonders by injecting ageing celebrities with cells scraped from the foetuses of lambs. This treatment, known as cellular therapy, was supposed to be able to cure every known disease to which the middle-aged are notoriously prone – heart disease, cancer, cirrhosis of the liver, depression, insomnia, impotence. For all I know it did wonders for your golf swing too.

Best news of all, especially to Maugham who had come more

and more to resemble a shrivelled walnut, was that it halted the advance of old age. The old boy fell for it, and shortly before the war hurried to the Niehans clinic at Clarens, near Vevey, on the shores of Lake Geneva.

If a few harmless jabs in the bum could work wonders for the likes of Thomas Mann, the Aga Khan (or the Gaga Khan, as one or two of his close friends had ribbingly started calling him), Pope Pius XII and Merle Oberon, then who, he argued, was he to deny himself a longer and a merrier life than the Almighty had obviously had in mind for him?

On arrival at the Chalet La Prairie, Maugham and his friend Alan Searle (who, although only thirty-four, was suffering a nasty skin complaint that Niehans thought he could probably deal with) were whisked off to the clinic's private slaughterhouse to view the pregnant ewes from whose unborn children the miracle serum was soon to be scraped and shot into our heroes' backsides. Up to ten injections at a time were administered. Not surprisingly the patients took a day or two to recover. One does not, after all, get younger every day of the week.

Tobacco and alcohol were strictly forbidden, which might explain why certain alcoholically-minded celebrities decided that even the rigours of old age were infinitely preferable to a few hours without a stiff brandy and soda.

The effects were, by all accounts, staggering. Mr Searle declared that he had never felt friskier in his life – for all the good it did him.

'Here I was,' he said later, 'with all this bull and lamb and whatnot in me, and I didn't know what to do with it.'

Maugham, at the age of sixty-four, was also feeling a new man – or rather he wasn't, since patients were strictly segregated following the treatment, presumably for that very reason. According to Mr Searle, the great man found himself 'with very distinct urges . . . usually in the bath'.

Sadly, while his body remained in excellent physical condition until well into old age, his brain failed to keep pace – hence the nightmare of his declining years in which no one, not even his own daughter, was immune from the rantings and ravings of his deranged mind.

Most of us have neither the money, the time, nor the inclination to go to such lengths to recapture our lost youth. Still, no one likes to give in to middle age without putting up some sort of fight. The question is, how far is one prepared to go in one's efforts to stave off the advancing years without making a complete fool of oneself?

Hair, Loss of

Of the several outward and visible manifestations of the onset of middle age, none is more obvious or, to the average sufferer, more distressing than the loss of one's hair.

Now before I go any further, I should like to make it perfectly clear that I have no axe to grind where hair is concerned; only a pair of kitchen scissors with which I occasionally tamper with the bits at the side of the neck when they start to curl round my ear lobes like bindweed and I haven't had time to make an appointment with my barber. In short, I am long on hair.

Never once, to my certain knowledge, have I stepped out of my bath to find the scum-line bristling with discarded capillaries. My brush and comb do tend to acquire a slightly hirsute look after a week of heavy action through the locks, but no more so than I remember from my schooldays.

My hairline shows no signs of receding nor has the crown of my head been subject at any time to unseasonal draughts.

No boasting, but a trichologist I visited recently to carry out an in-depth interview on the subject commented, after giving me a thorough going-over with a magnifying glass, than I have 'beautiful hair that will last for forty years'.

But what of those less fortunate than I? Why *do* they go bald? It's like this:

People's heads are pitted all over with tiny follicles or holes about $3/8$ inch deep. Nestling at the bottom of each of these is the papilla – the mother of the hair, as it were – which is connected with all the blood vessels and nerve endings and so on. (I had thought at this point of including a colour diagram, but in deference to those who happen to be reading this while eating, I have decided to leave it to the imagination.)

All of us lose hairs constantly. As soon as one falls out the papilla simply bangs up a replacement hair in no time. If, however, a follicle should for any reason close up, then the papilla will die and it will be an irreplaceable hair that bites the coat collar.

Most people go bald on the top of their heads or at the temples. This is because sex hormones called androgens circulating in the body affect the skin via androgen receptors – which doubtless gives rise to the popular theory (popular among baldies anyway) that baldness is a sign of excessive virility. My own theory, for what it's worth, is that if you are bald, you have got to try that much harder just to prove that you're not as old as you look.

Some men are lucky and get away with what is known in trichological circles as a 'transient moult'. In other words, a whole lot of hair falls out, rather like the cat's in the spring, and then grows back again. This would account for the apparent success rate of certain so-called baldness cures. On the whole, though, the baldy loses his hair up to a certain point and that's it. This will not grow back no matter how many thousands of pounds are spent on lotions and unguents, massages and electro-therapy sessions.

In fact there is only one cure for falling hair and that is castration – and even that won't bring back the hair that has already gone. It won't bring back a lot of other things either, and I would not on the whole advise it, especially for the man who is concerned about appearing attractive to women.

Male Pattern Baldness Reduction

This can be achieved in a number of different ways, each as scalp-crawlingly unattractive as the next.

You can have a square inch or two of your bald pate removed and the hair-fringed edges pulled towards each other and sewn together. This takes about an hour to do, and a man who hitherto looks as if he's just been shaved for a visit to the electric chair, walks away with a full head of thick, luxuriant hair – supposing, of course, that the rest of his hair was thick and luxuriant in the first place. This method is not recommended for very bald people indeed, unless they're very keen on the idea of wearing their ears on top of their heads.

For the man going bald at the front the flap graft is a strong possibility. This involves removing a strip of skin containing hair from the side of the head and laying it across the bald patch. This method does not, as you might suppose, leave you with an equally bald patch on one side, since the skin in the donor area, as we say in transplanting circles, is also pulled together and stitched.

A company called The Transform Clinic claim to be able to eliminate baldness in just three hours with a sensational new treatment from Los Angeles called Hair Speed. According to their literature, 'the visual effect and speed of improvement are so staggering as to be almost beyond belief.' However, I am not here to provide free advertising for any firm, let alone one in which I have no personal interest whatever. I'm sure they are perfectly capable of staggering you without my help.

Probably the best known method is the classic hair transplant, also known as punch grafting. This consists of removing little tufts from the back of the neck, punching small holes in the affected area with a thing like a potato gun, and jamming the little tufts in the resulting holes. A bit like planting carrots.

And that's exactly what it can look like, too, when it comes up a month or two later. On the other hand, if you're lucky, you can finish up looking like Frank Sinatra on a good night.

Given the choice, one can understand why so many baldies prefer to stay that way, and to hell with the jokes.

Wigs and Hairpieces

This is far and away the most popular way of covering up bald patches – from the seriously receding hairline to the full-scale shiny pate.

Even as you read these words, something like half a million men in Britain alone are shamelessly walking about on racecourses, eating *tournedos rossini* in expensive restaurants, chairing local authority planning meetings, kissing young women, playing in foursomes, having ding-dongs with traffic wardens, etc. etc. in the sure belief that their shame is cunningly and completely concealed from the eyes of a cruel and mocking world. Despite ever more sophisticated materials and techniques, the vast majority of wigs (or hairpieces as we must now learn to call them) seem to me to be no more convincing than the famous Crown Toppers of the fifties. Notable sporters of wigs and toupées of varying shapes and sizes include Reginald Bosanquet, the gravity-defying antics of whose lively pieces have over the years held a nation on the edge of its seat and vied with wars, revolutions, floods, strikes and disasters for sheer audience fascination; Sean Connery who is for ever being talked into hiding the top of his wispy sunburned skull beneath some unlikely bush or other – as if it made the slightest difference to *his* animal magnetism; David Niven, whose gradually receding wigs must surely one day earn him some sort of perukial award for verisimilitude beyond the call of mere duty;

and Ernie Wise, who always looks as though he's wearing a wig and may well be doing so for all I know, but almost certainly isn't, thereby earning himself the dubious honour of being the only man in showbusiness history to wear a phoney wig.

Happily, we are not as obsessed in this country with the need to look twenty-eight as they are in America, where a middle-aged man up for an executive job will do anything to prove that he is fifteen years younger than he really is, and will march into an interview wearing a rug that is about as convincing as Ronald Reagan playing Lear, rather than reveal the tiniest scrap of bare skin atop his nut.

And talking about Ronald Reagan, it's one thing to be prematurely red-haired, but when the rest of you looks only slightly younger than a Galapagos iguana, the overall effect has an eerily *Sunset Boulevard* feel to it (see Hair Dyes and Colourants).

Still, let's face it, men are pretty vain the world over and, according to Mr Hamilton of Wig Specialities Ltd ('Undetectable Toupées') of Seymour Street in London, literally thousands of unhappy baldies make their nervous way every year into his rather theatrical-looking Reception and spend anything up to £300 having a piece knocked up.

Since the average wig looks to me about as expensive as a piece of bathroom carpet picked up in a remnant sale and fitted by a colour-blind plumber, I could not resist raising a quizzical eyebrow at Mr Hamilton's fee.

However, all was explained when he pointed out that if people want to cut corners and wear cheap hair, they are very welcome to do so, but he is certainly not prepared to be a party to it.

Anyone, it seems, can pick up Chinese and Indian hair for a song, then bleach it and colour it something completely different. The only trouble is that dyed hair has this awkward habit of taking one look at sunlight and turning a nasty shade of gingery red.

Some people don't even use hair, preferring, like a milkman I know, to buy spools of nylon thread which they then cut to length and attach individually to their scalps with gum. Not only does it make them look perfectly ridiculous, but it takes so long that they have to get up at two o'clock in the morning to put it all on. They then spend most of the evening taking it all off again. (Hence, some people don't get their milk until lunchtime.)

No, if you want the real quality stuff – and let's face it, it's as hard to come by as good caviare these days – then you've got to expect to pay for it. I mean, for your best Swedish platinum blonde Sonray, you've got to be looking at anything between £20 and £40 an ounce.

On the other hand, they'll do you a perfectly workmanlike and very much cheaper line in Eastern Europe. Your Bulgarian peasant for example, comes out at only about £15 an ounce. Ditto your Yugoslavian, your Czechoslovakian, and your Sicilian Mountain.

But then, of course, in those parts, a lot of people make good pin money out of growing their hair specially to sell to hair merchants, and if it's a good, all-purpose switch you're after at a price you can afford, they do say that a nice length of novice nun takes a lot of beating.

I dread to think where one should go for a decent chest wig.

Mr Hamilton, whose Christian name is David ('not *the* David Hamilton,' he says with an embarrassed laugh) insists that, once attached to the skull with double-sided tape, his expensive middle-European creations are guaranteed never to blow off in a high wind, as per the old chestnut, and I'm inclined to believe him.

At the same time, were I ever to find myself in need of one of his head warmers, I would challenge him to promise me unconditionally that I could be absolutely certain of the damned thing never coming adrift in rather more unusual circumstances.

Stories of young ladies in bed with gentlemen not their husbands who have been put off sex, and men, for life upon waking in the morning, experiencing a curious tingling feeling and looking down to find what appears to be a large dead rat between the sheets, apocryphal though they may be, are believable enough to persuade me that one might do better to come clean and admit one's hairlessness from the word go.

The other problem with hair pieces is that, having finally wrenched the things agonisingly from the cranium, they instantly lose any recognisable shape, substance or, to the untrained eye, purpose, and are therefore in constant danger of being casually swept away along with any other rubbish one's wife/charlady/manservant/au pair girl may feel has no place in a clean and tidy house.

An actor friend of mine recently lashed out a three-figure sum or more on a cunning little piece of corn-coloured nonsense that wonderfully filled in a bald patch at the back of his head, making him look ten years younger.

One day I received a desperate telephone call from Heathrow saying that he had tried to ring his wife but hadn't managed to get hold of her and that, since he had a plane to catch, would I call her instead at the earliest possible opportunity because he had left his piece lying around somewhere in the flat and he was concerned that, as that was the day the cleaning lady came, it might get swept up with the rubbish.

I still suffer the occasional twinge of conscience to think that, had I managed to get hold of her a few minutes earlier . . . but I needn't go on.

She combed (no laughing, if you don't mind) the rubbish tips of south London for a week before finally admitting defeat.

Wisely, he has never bothered with a replacement. For his piece, I mean.

Other problems of a quite different and unexpected nature can arise. A barber I know recalls being telephoned by a customer complaining that his piece had shrunk dramatically in the rain. The truth, when it finally emerged, was that the man's wife had become so disgruntled at the dramatic new lease her husband's life had taken since acquiring his fresh head of hair and so bored at being left at home while he was out gallivanting with young women, that in a fit of pique she tore it off his head one day and hurled it into the washing machine.

In a TV programme about baldness that I once watched, a middle-aged man wearing quite the most ill-fitting, badly coloured and obvious wig I have ever seen outside an amateur theatrical group was complaining to the interviewer about the heartless comments insensitive people are inclined to make when faced with this alien growth.

'What sort of comments exactly?' enquired the interviewer politely.

'Well,' he replied. 'You know. Things like "It shows". Things like that.'

He said this in tones of such injured innocence that for a while I actually found myself feeling quite sorry for him. I mean, he really didn't know.

But then nine out of ten cheap wigs *do* show. They look terrible. They don't match. They don't fit. And the larger they are, the worse they look. I even heard of one man who wore his back to front for many years without realising it.

To be fair to Mr Hamilton, he does always suggest to his customers that they go for something small and subtle; it's they who insist on the full, thick, luxuriant mops that would look silly even on David Hamilton – *the* David Hamilton, that is.

The Hair Weave

For many years I laboured under the misapprehension that this was a type of cloth used in the manufacture of men's suiting. Indeed I felt sure that lengths of this material had been presented to me by various tailors over the years. 'How about the hair weave, sir? A hard-wearing, all-purpose cloth. Looks as much at home on the racecourse as in the board meeting. Very much your sort of style, if I may say so, sir, and among what I might call our medium price range materials.'

There are two types of hair weave. The first is merely a different way of attaching a wig or hairpiece to one's existing growth, if one (a) doesn't trust the standard method and (b) is unable to wear tape next to the skin.

What happens is this. The customer is attached via three threads to a sort of mini-telegraph pole. The weaver then makes a thin plait using the customer's own hair as a fourth thread. The plait is then tied tightly round the head and secured on the far side, and it is to this rather frail-sounding foundation that the wig is then woven, using upholstery needles and a basic blanket stitch.

Not surprisingly, the bald patch tends to sweat rather a lot during the warm weather. This results in itching, bad temper and a general disinclination to join in with such summer social activities as picnics, bathing parties and barbecues – hence the phrase 'He's a bit of a wet blanket'.

The other sort of hair weave involves a light net of silk or nylon which is laid over the bald patch. The hairs round the edge, plus any that might still be growing in the middle, are drawn through the net and knotted. Hairs are then woven into the anchored net, thus giving the impression of a full head of hair.

Hair weaves do have a distinct advantage over the ordinary wig in that they are practically impossible to dislodge and are there-fore enormously popular among all-in wrestlers, scientists work-ing in wind tunnels, and farmers who milk by hand.

On the other hand, the hair weaver does have to visit the hairdresser every time he wants his hair washed. Once every six weeks would appear to be about par for the course, provided your friends do not start making pointed comments about funny smells etc. first. Even so, it's likely to cost about £300 a year.

There are those who have been known to leave it even longer between washes, but this is not recommended since, as one's own hair grows, the wig begins to rise from the top of one's head like a hirsute soufflé, thus inviting passers-by to stare in the street and talent scouts to try to inveigle you on to embarrassing TV programmes. This is knows as the Brillo Effect and is one very good reason for leaving one's hair very much unwoven.

The Robinson Sweep

Named after its most famous exponent, the distinguished broadcaster Mr Robert Robinson, this method of cranium concealment consists of growing the hair on one side of one's head enormously long and then taking a parting about half an inch above the ear and combing the hair across one's bald area until it meets up with the other smaller bit on the other side.

There are various drawbacks to this technique, the most obvious being that, if the wind should suddenly gust at an unexpected moment, you cannot help but look very silly indeed, and in such an event, far from concealing one's baldness, the Sweep draws more attention to the fact than ever a bald head would.

Although popularised by one of our leading radio and television performers, the Robinson Sweep is not recommended for those planning to make a career as a TV interviewer or pundit, since most viewers devote so much time to puzzling out precisely where it is that the growth of hair begins and ends, that anything which anyone wearing it might have to say is more or less completely wasted.

This might well explain Mr Neil Kinnock's failure to become leader of the Labour Party. Mr Arthur Scargill's rise to the top of the union ladder is quite inexplicable.

(The *on dit* is that some interesting work is currently being done by the Department of Cosmetic Trichology at somewhere like the University of Tuscaloosa on a whole new method of growing the beard up over the top of the head, but these are early days and news of any serious breakthrough must await the second edition.)

Hair, Retention of

Luckily, as I mentioned earlier, I have a full – rather too full, some may say – head of hair and have no need to resort to any of these drastic means of camouflage. Which is not to say that I do not worry about my hair.

Any day now I could wake up to find that my entire thatch has transferred itself overnight to my pillow. Alopecia, they say, is a nervous disease that can attack anyone at any time, and who knows . . . ? A larger than usual telephone bill, a visit from the VAT man, a sinister knocking sound at around 55 mph, a ding-dong with the neighbour over the cat's do-es in the garden . . . any unusual worry or stress could bring it on at the most unexpected moment.

They also say that alopeciacs can often enjoy a full growth of new hair in the fullness of time. Like Duncan Goodhew, I suppose? Or the BBC radio producer who, after many years of hairlessness, is still known to his family as Radio Savalas?

If the middle-aged baldy thinks he's got problems, spare a thought for the middle-aged hairy for whom every stroke of the comb and squirt of the herbal shampoo may well be his last. Imagine how much time each day he must devote to worrying about ways of keeping the thatch he's got.

Convinced one day for no particular reason that I was wreaking irrevocable havoc with my hair by dampening it every morning with hard tap water, I hurried off to Kensington to seek the advice of an anonymous member of the Institute of Trichology.

Eight-thirty on a Thursday morning and his surgery was already buzzing with activity as white-coated girls anointed nervous heads – male and female – with strange unguents before plunging them beneath large drying lamps designed to break down the various ingredients of the lotions, thus forcing each one to tackle its special task on, under and around the customer's scalp.

The air was heavy with pungent and unnamable odours and it was with some relief that I was shown outside in the pouring rain and downstairs to the trichologist's rather dark consulting room.

A youthful sixty-three-year-old who had clearly survived middle age with barely a scratch to show for it and was evidently about to o'erleap old age in a similarly no-nonsense fashion, he began straightaway by knocking one old chestnut about baldness firmly on the head – viz: that loss of hair equals loss of virility equals complete failure to attract women.

'The fact is,' he said with the confident air of a man who speaks from personal experience, 'that losing your hair shouldn't make an atom of difference to your sex life. It's a sense of humour that counts with women. If you can make an eighteen-year-old laugh in a restaurant, she'll be far more interested in you than she ever will be with some handsome young Lothario with the best head of hair in the world.'

I didn't like to say anything, but in my not inconsiderable experience, trying to raise so much as a *smile* from an eighteen-year-old is about as likely as cracking witty with a yak about the life and times of Jean-Paul Sartre.

Still, I won't go on about that just at this moment. I think you'll find I've got quite enough to say about the middle-aged man and the younger woman in Chapter 12.

Suffice to say for now that (a) I have better things to do with the limited lifespan at my disposal than to spend it sitting about in restaurants eating overpriced food and wisecracking with bolshy teenagers on the outside chance of a spot of how's-your-father back in her shared flat in Camberwell, and (b) were I by some bizarre chance to find myself lounging around in a jacuzzi surrounded by a bathful of nubility, I'd still prefer to do so with as full a head of hair as possible. Dark brown for choice.

The trichologist could not have been more sympathetic, so much so that I feel it my duty to my fellow worriers to pass on some of his excellent advice.

Hair Dyes and Colourants

The man who is keen on appearing sexually attractive to women would be advised to give these a wide berth. Women actually like grey hair. Indeed, as I understand it, there are those who, at the merest hint of a grizzled temple, will tear their clothes off, hurl themselves upon the owner and start making exorbitant demands upon his amazed body to an extent unknown outside the pages of Dr Alex Comfort's *Joy of Sex*. (See Comfort, Dr Alex: *Ageing: the Biology of Senescence*.)

For those who would rather not leave things to chance, there are various concoctions on the market guaranteed to colour your ageing locks a youthful shade of dark brown.

Probably the best known of all is Grecian 2000. It certainly works. The only real drawback for the man who likes to wear his hair on the short side is that you do have to keep applying the stuff at regular intervals if you don't want your terrible secret revealed to the girls in the office.

There are those who still swear by Morgan's Pomade which middle-aged worriers have been rubbing into their heads for decades, despite the very real risk of a scalpful of blackheads.

These will not show, of course, if you are a black man. But then neither, I'm afraid, will certain tints and colourants.

Hair Tonics

I had a a rather racy friend at school in the mid fifties who enjoyed the sort of lifestyle that the rest of us could only dream of.

In the summer holidays he travelled to the South of France on the Blue Train and put up at Menton where he had intercourse with women. He lunched at the Dorchester and had his shoes made at Lobb's. Or at least he said he did.

I believed him. A boy of fifteen who puts Decker's Bay Rum on his hair is capable of anything. Most of us reckoned that what was good enough for Denis Compton was good enough for us and so larded our heads with handfuls of Brylcreem – that or some other hair tonic. Silvikrin or Vaseline for preference; otherwise any other concoction the barber cared to palm off on us. Since the majority of so-called tonics comprise 10 per cent methylated spirits and 30 per cent water, I doubt if they did our hair a lot of good. Or, for that matter, a great deal of harm.

Water

You should avoid dampening your hair with tap water. It contains calcium salts which can cause scaling.

So there you are. I had a feeling I was making a terrible mistake. Is it any wonder my hair sometimes looks like the inside of a kettle?

Dandruff

Like BO, halitosis, blackheads, excessive nose and ear hair and ubiquitous, ill-concealed razor nicks, merely another outward manifestation of the middle-aged Englishman's inner conviction, usually engendered by his wife, that no one's going to look at him after the age of forty, so why bother? Those that think otherwise should simply consider changing their shampoo.

Desperate Measures

There are, it would seem, no lengths to which men will not go in an effort to retain their hair. Anything that can possibly be smeared on, rubbed in or sprinkled over it has been tried – including margarine, onions, soot, mustard and paraffin. Now there's something that might make an eighteen-year-old laugh.

Eyesight, Failing

Now here, I must confess, I have a personal problem. It first came to my attention about six months ago. I was sitting in bed late one evening reading Anthony Powell, as one does when one gets to my age (see Reading Matter for the Middle Aged who are Panicked by the Realisation that there is the Whole of English Literature to get through in about Twenty-five Years and they'd Better Make a Start Somewhere), when . . .

But hold hard. In order to appreciate the full impact that the dramatic turn of events I am about to describe had on me, I must go back some thirty-five years and fill in the background with a potted account of my opthalmological history.

It all began on the day my parents and I were invited by some kindly neighbours to pop in and watch a television broadcast of the 1948 Olympic Games from Wembley. It was when I found that I was unable to distinguish between the well-known Jamaican sprinter Arthur Wint and Mrs Attlee that my parents decided that all was not well. The fact that the screen was only about six inches across and the picture about as clear as a pointillist painting by Seurat did not in the least sway them in their opinion that I was badly in need of glasses.

The following morning they drove me to the village where I had my eyes tested in the gloomy back room of the local chemist's. There was not a wonderful choice of frames available to NHS patients in 1948. If you were a small boy, you either had a black wire frame or a black wire frame. These were completely round, were known universally as giglamps and made the wearer look like a double victim of the classic soot and telescope joke (see How to Keep up with the Children). The only advantage to be gained from wearing specs as far as I could see (no joke intended) was that they could be used as an excuse (not always very effective) for getting out of being bashed up by evil-minded village boys.

Thirty years passed without any noticeable change in my powers of vision. Occasionally I would alter my frames to suit my changing image and to bring them in line with current fashion.

In 1974, in an uncharacteristic show of conceit, and under the influence of the then editor of the *Sunday Times*, Mr Harold Evans, I treated myself to a pair of contact lenses. He and I were skiing together in the French Alps at the time and the effect of youthfulness and vigour that lenses quite clearly created upon this myopic forty-four-year-old won my vote straight away. Ditto the confidence with which he skied, although a comparative beginner (see Hobbies and Activities, The Middle-Aged Man's).

Unfortunately, the representative of the contact lens firm into whose hands I so blithely put myself suffered from such skin–searing halitosis (see Unfortunate Afflictions, Middle-Aged Men's) that when I stepped out of the shop for a short trial walk round the block wearing a pair of practice lenses I felt quite groggy. I was also half blinded by the tears which streamed continuously from my eyes and, before I knew what, I had gone hard into a lamp post, bringing up a bruise the size of a pullet's egg above one eye and dislodging the lens which disappeared some-where up inside the lid. For all I knew it was at that very moment working its way remorselessly through my brain. Funnily enough I was beginning to feel a little on the headachy side.

Worse was to come, however, since I obviously must have suffered some obscure form of Pavlovian reaction, so that when my new lenses finally arrived, the moment I attempted to put them in I was reminded of the rep's halitosis and felt quite unwell for half an hour or more. I was never able to approach them with any degree of enthusiasm again. Nor, on the few occasions on which I did manage to get them in and out again, did I ever succeed in doing so without the aid of a large, well-lit mirror – a fact that more than once led to humiliating scenes on the ski slopes.

Later I settled for a neat compromise by wearing lightweight steel frames with plastic lenses known in America, I believe, as aviator glasses.

The point of this potted, not to say as cooked-in-a-slow-oven-with-herbs-and-spices, account of my life and times with the eye-testing board is that for me glasses were for years much more to do with fashion and looks than with medicine. Thus, while I have always been vaguely aware of the fact that an important part of my physical equipment is defective and that it is only by wearing glasses that I am able to do all those things that physically perfect people take for granted, I have been using these opthalmological crutches for so many years now that I take the fact of satisfactory vision very much for granted. In a way, I suppose I'm rather like the late Sir Douglas Bader.

For the middle-aged man, on the other hand, who has enjoyed perfect vision all his life and suddenly realises one day that, however far away he holds the restaurant menu, the words are still blurred and unreadable, the business of wearing spectacles is a different matter altogether.

The first problem he must face is that of admitting that he is suffering from that most common of middle-aged afflictions known as short-sightedness. There is obviously some perfectly simple solution, he tells himself, and everyone else: the poor standard of modern print, fluorescent lighting in the office, pollution, arms getting shorter etc. For those who resolutely refuse to admit that the inevitable has at last occurred there are one or two possible escape routes.

In cases of real emergency one can always borrow the wife's glasses. This has the advantage (a) of making one appear rather charmingly eccentric and (b) of affording one a free joke or two at the expense of the wife. A serious disadvantage, however, is that it (a) provides conclusive proof of one's short-sightedness and (b) gives the wife another excuse to complain that she can never find anything when you are in the house and why don't you leave things where they are instead of going round tidying all the time? But even when one does at last give in and takes the dreaded step through the optician's doorway, is there any way in which one can be sure of carrying off the fact of having to wear reading glasses with some degree of *élan*?

The half-moon spectacles seem to have gained a certain amount of ground among the middle-aged professional classes in recent years. Although on the one hand their sheer old-fashioned

Dickensian appearance can easily transform a mere middle-aged man into a comparatively ancient individual (see Kennedy, Senator Edward), when worn with the right spirit of affectation, their innate whimsicality can imbue certain men with a degree of humour which would otherwise be entirely lacking. Half-moons (National Health ones anyway) also have the advantage of costing half the price of full-moons and there is many a niggardly advertising executive and parsimonious PR man peering over the top of his specs at this very moment, creating for himself a reputation for wit and style for entirely the wrong reasons.

Good old-fashioned, heavy tortoiseshelly-looking reading glasses can also create a more interesting effect then might at first appear. Real tortoiseshell is obviously a plus for those wishing to make a public point concerning their worldly success, provided that success is solid enough to pay for them in the first place. The real problem, however, is not the cost (£100 minimum before you have even begun to think about lenses etc.) but the fact that nine out of ten people cannot tell the difference between real and imitation tortoiseshell anyway. And since the wearer runs a very real risk of being cast out of polite society as a blatant anti-conservationist, he would never dare tell people that they are real and therefore the whole point of this expensive exercise is nullified before it has even begun.

Aviator glasses can certainly create a youthful impression, if you fancy to looking like Cliff Richard, but for the long-sighted they have the distinct disadvantage of being difficult to whip off and use in a dramatic way to make a point at a strategic moment during a meeting or interview (see Kennedy, Ludovic). As body language goes, this particular form of punctuation really only works with classic executive frames. Ditto chewing the earpiece during reflective moments. On the other hand, too much whipping off and chewing can cause even the strongest frame to snap at the side at unfortunate moments, hence a whole new line in glasses with sprung joints which, according to my optician, are 'all the go' these days.

But to return to me in bed with Anthony Powell. There I was reading away when it suddenly occurred to me that I could not read more than two or three sentences without feeling an overwhelming urge to lay the book down on my chest and close my eyes.

All sorts of possible explanations flashed through my mind: Penguin Books had started using a much smaller typeface; the bulb in the bedside lamp needed upping from 40 to 60 watts; I had developed a hitherto undiscovered aversion to Mr Powell's literary style; I was going blind . . .

It was only when in a desperate moment I removed my glasses that I realised that not only was I still as short-sighted as I had been at the age of eight, but that I was now long-sighted as well. Simultaneously, a terrible word began to form itself in my mind – bifocals.

My optician could not have been more sympathetic if he'd tried. As a fellow sufferer, he knew only too well how I felt, and said that I should think myself lucky I don't work in a British Rail Information Office. Passenger timetables, like National Health Service forms, are quite obviously designed by young people who have not the faintest conception of the problems they create for many over the age of forty-two. Is it any wonder so many of us are caught out by Hire Purchase Agreements and Holiday Booking Forms? It isn't that we *haven't* read the small print we *can't* read it.

Having thoroughly engaged my sympathies, he went on to say that he quite understood my reluctance to countenance bifocals, and so did the manufacturers, which is why more and more middle-aged bats are taking to wearing things called multifocals. These work on the same principle as bifocals except that the lens progresses in a gradual transition from near vision to distance vision.

In the words of one leading manufacturer: 'Not only are you assured of perfect near-vision, but you continue seeing clearly as you look up.' (It also presumably means you don't keep measuring your length across people's hallways as you misjudge the height of the front doorstep.) 'In a restaurant, for instance, you can read a menu and a label on a bottle of wine, or tell the time from a clock on the wall,' (a combination of skills which it has long been my fervant wish to master).

The multi-focal, according to the brochure, is 'the ideal lens for dynamic people who are obliged, because of their activities, to constantly and rapidly shift their attention from near to distant objects'. Quite what activities the writer had in mind I cannot think. The idea that dynamism should presuppose an unusual amount of eye movement is one that had never struck me before. Still, I daresay anyone who hopes to do well in the world of high finance or international business would be advised to keep a weather eye open at all times, if only to avoid the knives that are constantly about to be plunged into his back.

Speaking as a moderately dynamic person who rarely finds himself called upon to read wine labels and look at clocks simultaneously, I would recommend – and I think my optician would probably bear me out here – the simple and inexpensive expedient of raising one's glasses perhaps three-quarters of an inch when reading a wine label and dropping them back onto the bridge of one's nose the instant one wishes to know if the time has come to drink the stuff. Beyond that, I have little to offer fellow presbyopics but my profound sympathy.

Nose, Hairs up the

Hirsute nostrils are considered by certain types of women to be sexually attractive in some way that completely escapes me, and are therefore cultivated with enthusiasm in some more exotic corners of the globe.

Unfortunately, the hairy nose rarely comes off in the case of most Englishmen, being allied more closely with the generally lackadaisical approach to looks, appearance, clothes etc. which so many of us go to such enormous lengths to cultivate (see Coat Collars, Dandruff on the; Underarm Deodorants, Unfortunate Aversion of Middle-Aged Englishmen to; Suits, Smelly Old Favourite; and Heads, Black – passim).

Thus, what a veritable harvest home of hair protruding from the nostrils may gain in terms of animal magnetism, it all too often loses in general lack of hygiene. Imagine how you would feel if you were lying in someone's arms having recently explored their back teeth and looked up only to be confronted by something looking like a rubbish tip in the Black Forest?

On the whole, therefore, I would recommend regular grooming of the nostrils. Given that so many barbers have given up this useful and inexpensive sideline, this must be considered on the whole as a do-it-yourself exercise. There are various methods:

1. Scissors. Ideal provided you can work out from the reverse image in the mirror what you are supposed to be snipping at and where. Otherwise self-inflicted lacerations and nosebleed can all too often be the order of the day.

2. Razor, Safety. Can work wonders on exposed areas of nostril near centre section but can lead to total removal of entire portions if not very carefully controlled.

3. Razor, Electric. There are very few models on the market that will fit with any degree of comfort inside the average male nostril; however, attachment for sideboards perfectly satisfactory depending on how far hair protrudes.

4. Tweezers. Effective but eye-watering. Not recommended for wearers of contact lenses.

5. Fingers. Marginally cheaper than tweezers and marginally less effective, especially when fingers and/or nasal hair wet.

Teeth and Dentures

Here again I must declare an interest. All my life I have suffered a mouthful of the ugliest, most misshapen collection of pegs ever to be seen outside a dental museum.

I say 'all my life', but of course for all I know, my milk teeth may have been as regular and white and attractive as the Cow and Gate baby's.

The trouble started very soon after the war when my parents, well-intentioned as always, delivered me and my somewhat over-burgeoning second teeth into the hands of a local dentist. Quite how a man of his experience and qualifications could seriously have believed that it was possible to force so many teeth into quite such a small area baffles me to this day – not to say every dentist I have ever visited since.

His plan apparently was to fit me with a pink plastic plate divided at some strategic point by a screw with a little hole in it, and once a week, with the help of a small metal key, I was to give a turn on this screw, as a result of which my teeth would be forced into position.

In short, this did not work. Some teeth grew up behind others; other were pushed in or out at bizarre angles; a few grew more or less straight. I'd have done better to wear a set of teeth from a joke shop.

Still, looking back over the years I do not believe my life was too greatly affected. Had my early ambitions to become a film star in the Richard Todd mould ever been realised, I daresay my uneven smile could have let me down during the occasional screen test. But I cannot remember ever experiencing the slightest difficulty in chewing up tough steak or smoking a pipe in a masculine way or even removing the tops off ginger beer bottles.

A year or two ago I remember examining a dental x-ray which appeared to indicate that I was walking round with a mouthful of nothing but amalgam, and on one occasion an ex-naval dentist made such a bosh go of a root canal filling somewhere in the nether regions that in the end the whole thing had to be wrenched out.

But I couldn't complain. There I was, forty-three years old, with all my own teeth (or at least, all my own amalgam), which was more than many men of my age could boast.

And then, by way of research for this book, I went to interview this dentist in Mount Street. (Again professional etiquette prevents me from naming him, although should any of my readers feel, after reading this chapter, that Mr X is the answer to their dental dreams, then I feel sure that a discreet letter to me via my publishers, enclosing a nominal contribution towards my dental costs, would result in the information they desire.)

He spoke generally at first about modern dental methods (or 'supervised neglect' as he prefers to call it).

'It's all a matter of priorities,' he said in a deadpan Australian accent. 'People's teeth are worse in this country than almost anywhere else, because they think that video tape recorders are essential and teeth aren't.'

Oddly enough, I have been struck myself by how many people I have come across recently with shelves full of recordings of *Fawlty Towers* and terrible halitosis.

A dental fact that had hitherto escaped my notice, however, is that most tooth decay occurs before the age of twenty-five. After that, it's largely a matter of re-doing old fillings that have cracked or crumbled or, in some cases, fallen out altogether. As a friend of mine was once told by his dentist, 'Well, you'll have no more trouble with tooth decay. All we have to start worrying about now is your gums.'

Another even more startling fact, however, is that one's face is the exact upside down replica of one of one's front teeth – which would go a long way towards explaining why I look like a misshapen potato.

But is there anything one can do at my advanced age, I asked him, to improve one's general aspect, or has one left it all far too late? Could he, in other words (and I emphasised that I was putting this to him in a purely theoretical way) make me look younger than I really am?

Dentists, unlike doctors and motor mechanics who 'can't

promise you anything', tend to be enormously calm and reassuring, and Mr X was more so than most.

'Of course,' he said.

I laughed nonchalantly and said that, supposing, just supposing
I were a prospective patient coming to him for advice, what would
his view be of my dental state of affairs and what would he
recommend be done about it?

He said that he could tell something was wrong the moment I
walked in. 'You've forgotten how to smile properly, haven't you?'
he said. 'You're like a patient I had who was so self-conscious
about his teeth that he always spoke out of the corner of his
mouth. You give a quick half-smile, then close your mouth again
before anyone notices you've got a problem.'

This was certainly news to me and, by way of proving that he
was talking out of the back of his head, treated him to one of my
famous broad grins.

'Yes,' he said. 'I'm not surprised. The front two are more or
less okay. The next two you can't see at all because they're set
back and in shadow. Dracula-type eye-teeth are thought by many
people to be very sexy; you can take that any way you want. The
next two would be fine if you weren't missing one of them. As a
result you have nothing for the bottom one to bite against and in
time it will grow up into the cavity above so that you won't be able
to move your jaw any other way than open and shut. In addition to
which, if you should by any chance lose that one remaining back
tooth, you'll be straight into a plate situation . . .'

Some dentists, I have noticed, have an unfortunate habit of
taking brutal honesty a little too far at times and I'm afraid I had to
cut him short.

'Given,' I said rather tersely, 'that my dental future is at best
uncertain and at worst non-existent, what, theoretically speaking,
would you do about it?'

'Two crowns at the front,' he said. 'Bring those forward. Two
crowns and a bridge at the back.'

'How much?' I said. His no-nonsense antipodean manner was
beginning to rub off on me.

'Two hundred a unit,' he said.

I said, 'But that's a thousand pounds.'

He shrugged. 'Depends how much value you place on your
teeth,' he said.

'Are you saying,' I said, 'that I could be into a denture
situation?'

He shrugged again, non-commitally.

'The longer you leave it, the more expensive it becomes,' he said. 'In middle age, things like crowns and bridges are not so much cosmetic as functional. At the same time, they are unde-tectable, they make you look younger, better, fresher; you gain confidence, which in turn encourages you to open your mouth and lips and gives you a good posture and a nice smile.'

I said, 'And if I leave it and have to have dentures?'

He said, 'I can always build up a set of dentures in such a way that all those lines round your mouth and the creases at the corners of your lips are eliminated.' And by way of demonstration he jammed a couple of cotton wool pads between my cheeks and gums.

The effect was startling. Suddenly, I looked exactly like my two-and-a-half-year-old son. My skin was smooth, my cheeks were full, the years had dropped away from me and suddenly I was a young man again. For two pins I'd have settled for spending the remainder of my life padded out with cotton wool, were it not for the fact that when I spoke I sounded like a man talking through cotton wool. I prepared to thank him for his help and leave.

Quite how the subject of the National Health Service arose in relation to crowns and bridges I cannot now remember. All I do know is that, when I finally left, it was in the certain knowledge that, if everything went to plan and his recommendations were accepted by the powers-that-be, I would very soon be the proud possessor of four crowns and a bridge, a smile like David Essex, confidence I had not known for nearly forty years, and youthful looks that I assumed had gone for ever in about 1963 – and all for a mere £90.

I do not propose to hold up the story at this exciting stage with the bizarre correspondence between my dentist and the National Health Service regarding the merits and otherwise of my case. Suffice to say that a fortnight later I was in the chair and work was in progress.

The fear implied at one stage by an NHS official that, unless they examine each case presented to them with an exaggerated attention to detail, vast hordes of unworthy patients will be rushing forward and taking advantage of the system just for the fun of it, very soon proved itself to be entirely without foundation.

I was faintly amused at having great wadges of pink mould jammed up against my teeth, despite the foul taste and the sharp pain in my jaw caused by having to open my mouth so inordinately wide. But the drilling was a different matter altogether. It wasn't the pain that upset me, since this man's injections are unequalled for efficiency in the dental world. It was the sudden shock at realising that there I was, deliberately encouraging someone to remove a part of me that was alive and in full working order and irreplaceable. I can imagine similar thoughts passing through the mind of a man undergoing a vasectomy operation (see Vasectomy, The Middle-Aged Man's Guide to).

And then another thought struck me (see Irrational Fears, The Middle-Aged Man's Susceptibility to). What if the man didn't know what he was doing? What if, by some terrible quirk of fate, I had committed myself into the hands, not of a superb technician as I had supposed, but of a complete cowboy, whose magnificently appointed premises had been acquired through successful speculation on the Stock Exchange and *who wasn't really a dentist at all?*

Sweat started out on the palms of my hand. Just my luck that I should have been the sort of person who can never get anything done in this world without having to ring up afterwards and get someone round to do it again. And just when I thought I'd sorted out the business of the new kitchen floor.

'I could show you what your stumps look like,' the dentist said at last, 'but I can promise you, they're not a pretty sight.' I declined his invitation. It was too late to start fussing now.

The next stage was to fit me with a pair of temporary caps which he did with astonishing rapidity. At the same moment he produced a small hand mirror.

'Look at that,' he said. 'Ten years younger.'

The effect was startling. It is given to few of us in this life to alter our appearances in a matter of seconds, and it is an experience I can thoroughly recommend.

It was unfortunate that, thanks to the paralysing efficiency of the injection, I was unable to raise my upper lip quite as revealingly as I would have liked. However, by dint of superhuman willpower I managed to achieve a semi-Bogartian sneer which I felt convinced would stand me in excellent stead with women for years to come.

This newfound confidence was, I am sorry to say, shortlived, since the moment the injection wore off I became enormously self-conscious of these new shapes which appeared to press against my upper lip and over my lower lip to such a marked degree that, despite constant reassurance from every mirror, I became convinced that I looked exactly like George Formby. Or worse, Mike *and* Bernie Winters rolled into one.

It didn't help that when I arrived home, the mother's help, a normally perceptive and observant eighteen-year-old, failed to notice any difference in my appearance whatsoever.

'Go on,' I said, supposing that she was playing some sort of game with me. 'You're not trying.'

'I don't understand what you mean,' she said.

'All right,' I said. 'I'll give you a clue.'

'Film, TV or book?' she said.

'Above the waist,' I said.

'You've put on a clean shirt.'

'Ask me to smile,' I said.

'Smile,' she said.

I gave her the full piano.

'Oh, of course,' she said. 'I've got it. You've had your hair cut.'

I told her she was getting warmer. But that was the best she could do unaided, so finally I pointed in an exaggerated way at my mouth.

'Gracious,' she exclaimed. 'Someone's given you two false teeth.'

Even now, some two months after acquiring my five new teeth and despite the care with which Mr X chose just the right shade of grey to match my old ones, I still suffer a little from self-consciousness. I had hoped that my air of modesty might prove an endearing quality as far as women are concerned, but so far there is little evidence to support the theory that men with good teeth are noticeably more sexually attractive than those without. On the other hand, I feel certain that the presence in one's mouth of some clean new teeth must cut down the possibility of that most unfortunate of middle-age afflictions – halitosis.

For those who should happen to fall prey to this, the ultimate in antisociability, I cannot recommend dental floss highly enough. A length of this lightly-waxed cotton drawn gently through the gaps between one's teeth once or twice a day can work wonders should you ever wonder why it is that everyone you speak to seems to be suffering from a heavy cold and holding handkerchiefs to their noses.

However, it is recommended that one tooth be flossed at a time. The amusing revue sketch I once saw performed, in which a man demonstrated how it is possible to weave a long length of floss along a complete row of teeth and with one sharp movement clean all of them and finished up by pulling out the whole lot, has more truth to it that one might suppose.

Persistent sufferers may like to be reminded that some of the greatest men in the history of the world enjoyed a history of bad breath (e.g. Clark Gable, Bertrand Russell, Rembrandt) and if it ever affected the success they enjoyed with women, then I certainly do not recall hearing about it.

Hearing and Deaf Aids

I cannot speak from personal experience here, but I am assured that, if brought discreetly into play at the right moment, the phrase 'I'm sorry. I'm a little deaf. A legacy from my SAS days, you know,' can achieve astonishing results. Depending on *how* you phrase the words, it can encourage interesting people to speak a little louder and bores to shut up completely. Of course, it can work the other way round. The onus is entirely on you.

Ear trumpets are recommended only for middle-aged novelists anxious to acquire a reputation for eccentricity and crustiness. In the long run this can prove to have more good financial sense to it than may at first appear, although not always for the immediate family of the deaf novelist concerned.

Pin and Tuck Jobs

The idea that, with a quick and painless application of the surgeon's knife, followed by a few harmless stitches, one can in an instant recover one's lost looks, if not one's youth, does not appeal as strongly to middle-aged men whose faces are falling apart as it does to women. Not in this country anyway. In California, which appears to be largely populated by fifty-year-old swingers in open Porsches and figure-hugging shirts to the navel, swathed in gold and tangled grey body hair, remarrying once a year, cavorting in discotheques every night, and sniffing exotic substances through tightly rolled bank notes approximately every hour and a half, there are men who will treat themselves to several thousand dollars' worth of cosmetic work as casually as they will change their wife for a newer, faster model.

All too often, however, at the first sign of the scalpel the wrinkles appear to head south and cluster together for protection in the general area of the neck, thus giving the unwitting patient the look of a turkey who's laying a difficult egg. This is in no way meant to imply that the present President of the United States has undergone plastic surgery; merely that people who do often finish up looking like him.

In fact, the turkey effect can be removed by dint of a form of cosmetic surgery known as a Wattle Job. However, like the man who has been on a skiing holiday and returns with a very brown face and neck which contrasts startlingly with his very white body and limbs, the fellow who goes in for the complete face and wattle treatment would be advised not to remove his clothes in public – and in some cases in private – if he does not wish to give the impression of one who has had a complete head transplant.

Englishmen are, on the whole, deeply suspicious – and rightly so – of the man who chucks away good money on this sort of enterprise. It smacks too much of self-regard.

Still, the human mind will always attempt to prevail over human matter, and for those middle-aged men who feel that, in the memorable words of Dr Richard Gordon's uncle, 'If you're doing badly paint the cart', here is a very short list of technical expressions which they might care to bring out in their preliminary interview with the 'plastic surgeon' from Finchley whose name they have picked from an advertisement in a posh Sunday newspaper, in the hope of persuading him that they at least know what they are talking about. (Serious surgeons working as consultants to hospitals will almost certainly not entertain purely cosmetic cases. They have their time cut out treating real wounds and genuine deformities.)

Face Lift: The classic beauty operation whereby the surgeon makes an incision under cover of the hairline, pulls the facial skin taut, puts in a tuck and cuts off the remains. If performed too many times, a patient could end up with his tummy button up his nose.

Blepharoplasty: The operation that takes away the bags under your eyes, the better to allow them to open in stunned disbelief at the subsequent bill.

Mentoplasty: In which a lump of plastic is implanted in the area where chinless wonders should have chins. For those with an irrational and uncontrollable desire to look like Tommy Cooper.

Hair Transplant: See Transplant, Hair.

Chemical Peel: Not a round of Grandsire Triples rung by a group of campanological Boots employees but a hair- (not to say skin-) raising method of burning the wrinkles off the face with strong chemicals, or possibly with a rotating wire brush. For those who fancy a complexion like a brick wall.

Breast Enlargement: Not applicable, except in certain bizarre circumstances which I do not intend to discuss here. (See Ashley, April.)

Nose Job: See O'Toole, Peter.

Ear Job: A friend of mine with a pair of phenomenal jug-likes went in for this in his early forties. He was tired of being the only man he knew who could wind-surf without a sail (as opposed to this Daredevil Author who usually does it without a board either). His sleek, new, swept-back, go-ahead looks have helped his career no end, even though his wife still doesn't recognise him in the street.

As one who has suffered all his life from slightly sticky-out ears which I attempt to conceal with longish hair (a device that works reasonably well until some fool of a barber takes it into his head to snip a little more off the side than I have suggested (see Hair and Haircuts) and also from a modest, though nonetheless irritating, double chin, I have been tempted on more than one occasion to lay my head upon the chopping block. But I know deep down that I'd never actually get as far as the surgeon's waiting room. This is partly because I am notoriously mean where it comes to spending money on myself, but mainly because I really couldn't be bothered. You may appear to be able to prolong your youth for a year or two, but no one can prolong his life. As Richard Gordon commented re his uncle's cart-painting theory, 'Unhappily, the same broken-winded old horse, progressively enfeebled with the staggers and botts, must lug the gaudy caravan along the paths of glory which lead but to the grave, up increasingly steep hills.'

In which I take a thorough, if jaundiced,
look at the whole subject of body
maintenance and exercise – jogging,
marathon running, Royal Canadian Air
Force exercises, health clubs, rowing
machines, Bullworkers etc., and consider
the pros and cons of various sports and
games played by middle-aged men.

Chapter Three

I blame the *Sunday Times* myself.
For years middle-aged men had been unfit and overweight.
Middle-age spread is, after all, an inevitable and not particularly
unpleasant part of the ageing process. There's nothing to be done
about it except to find oneself a decent tailor who understands
about these things and to stop trying to squeeze into clothes that
are too tight and twenty years too young. I do not believe that I am
very different from the majority of men of my age, and when I
confess that I have never really been fit since the age of five and
declare that I see no reason, nearly forty years later, to attempt to
invest my body with qualities that it never possessed in the first
place, I feel sure that most of my generation would throw their
hats in the air and seriously consider voting for me as the next
Minister of Health, if not Prime Minister.

And yet I know and they know that I am just being silly and
unfashionable and provocative, to be placed among the ranks of
such popular anti-exercisers as Robert Morley, Robert Robinson
and the like, rather than at the forefront of serious medico-
philosophical thought.

And why? Because half a dozen years ago, the *Sunday Times*
with its usual middle-class (and middle-aged) campaigning zeal,
took it upon itself to announce to the world that fitness is good for
you.

It did this in a series of colour magazine features entitled 'Body
Maintenance', which it later collected into a highly successful

book. It even wheeled in Dr David Owen to write a foreword to the book. In his best bedside manner he reminded us that 'coronary disease causes 43 per cent of all deaths in Britain among men aged forty-five to sixty-four'. He went on to pinpoint the causes: smoking cigarettes, overweight, high blood pressure, high blood-fat levels, lack of exercise . . .

'It is also well known,' he declared, 'that people who take regular and vigorous exercise usually enjoy better health and have lower blood-pressure and blood cholesterol levels.'

Lack of exercise, he concluded, 'is one of the besetting sins of modern men and women'.

Mea culpa, said I to that. The good doctor may never persuade me that the SDP is good for me, but his arguments on behalf of good healthy outdoor exercise and no more pork pies for lunch caught my vote straight away.

Curiously enough, I had remained impervious to all that scaremongering talk a few years ago about too many boiled eggs blocking up your arteries, and white sugar making your teeth fall out, and the importance of polyunsaturates, whatever they may have been when they were in vogue.

But then it takes the *Sunday Times* with its clever charts and diagrams and Brobdignagian close-up photographs and its air of cheerful doom to put the wind up the average middle-aged, middle-class sceptic like me.

One look at the graph showing that 25 per cent of those in Britain aged forty-five will never survive to collect their pension was enough to have me rummaging around in the loft for my old gym shoes and ringing up the Council Offices in Wandsworth for details about yoga classes. The fact that the Americans, the Scots and the Finns stand even less chance of surviving middle age than we do did not cheer me one little bit.

I decided to start off with something simple, like jogging.

Jogging

At first I seriously considered going the whole hog and kitting myself out with a matching track-suit (red preferably, for cheerfulness) and a proper pair of jogging shoes. However, I cannot see the point of spending good money on something until one knows for certain that it is definitely for one, and frankly a pair of jeans and a pullover fitted the bill perfectly adequately to my way of thinking. As did my gym shoes. They had seen me through five years at school without any problems and I could not see that a couple of broken eye-holes and a slightly crumbling inner sole justified my repaying their loyal service with a life sentence in the dustbin. A couple of coats of blanco had them looking as good as new in no time, and really the hole in the bottom of the right-hand shoe looked far worse than it really was.

It was a pity that the day I had chosen for my first jog should have dawned quite so grey and damp, and in the circumstances I think I was quite right to have called it off and gone back to bed for another hour. One's body obviously cannot benefit if one is not properly attuned mentally at the same time, as was proved the following morning when I set off across Battersea Park opposite the block of flats where I was living at the time, in glorious warm sunshine.

Although it was many years since, as a schoolboy, I had last moved at anything swifter than a saunter, I found that I quickly fell into the rhythm of rubber on tarmac and, as I pattered along the paths between the trees, my heart sang for sheer joy along with the birds and the distant sound of air traffic heading for Heathrow Airport.

I was surprised and interested to notice how very quickly I seemed to get out of breath. One is always hearing of middle-aged men suffering cardiac arrest as a result of too much sudden violent exercise, so I thought it prudent to pause as often as possible and rest on one of the many park benches. Even so, I found I was quite dizzy. Perhaps I should have had a small snack or a glass of milk before setting out. I made a mental note to check with my *Book of Body Maintenance* on this count the moment I got home.

Quite how I managed to tread in the dog do-es I can't think. I must have done it when I thought to vary my style of running by cutting across an area of grass and dodging about a bit through the wooded area in the middle. I have heard it said that people who jog too much on hard surfaces can suffer from a cracked pelvis.

I tried to clean it off as best I could on a patch of grass but it proved to be of that particularly adhesive variety that one seems to get rather a lot round SW11. Rather than waste any more time, I trotted across to the lake and swizzled the sole of my shoe across the surface of the water, only to remember that that was the shoe with the hole in it.

How on earth we town dwellers are expected to exercise

ourselves and generally maintain our bodies when we have to compete for space with incontinent curs, I cannot imagine. There was no mention of that, I noticed, in the *Sunday Times* book. I'd have thought that, purely from a health point of view if no other, they'd have included a trenchant paragraph or two on the subject of turd avoidance. It makes one wonder if any of these do-gooding journalists have ever actually practised what they so fervently preach.

Be that as it may, it is not easy to jog with a bruised knee, and by the time I had fully recovered, the motivation and the incentive had vanished – probably for ever.

On the other hand, I feel that my first-hand experience as a member of the jogging community, brief and inglorious though it may have been, does qualify me to make one or two points about this fashionable pastime which has obsessed the entire civilised world more thoroughly even than sex did in the sixties.

Point 1: Jogging is merely a euphemism for what I and my generation of schoolboys in the fifties knew as 'going for a run'. Aside from those of our more athletic schoolfellows who were members of the school cross-country team, the rest of us went for runs for one of two reasons: (a) as a form of compulsory exercise when bad weather had put the rugger pitch *hors de combat*, and (b) as a punishment. Runs were, therefore, never undertaken with the slightest degree of pleasure. From my recent experiences, I have no reason to suppose that, by disguising this dreary, boring and thoroughly unwelcome activity beneath the veneer of middle-class fashion, it makes it any the more pleasurable or useful an activity. As a schoolboy I never felt any better for going for a run; as a man, on the threshold of middle age, jogging makes me feel considerably worse.

Point 2: Our charming London parks are disfigured enough as it is with litter, vandalised trees and dog dirts without one's pleasure being further diminished by the sight of an endless parade of overweight, over-exposed figures in shorts (often worn mysteri-ously *over* tights) and gym shoes, puffing and panting their way through the landscape with their red, perspiring faces, their wob-bling pink flesh and their flabby backsides. In fact so strongly do I feel about it that I am seriously considering getting up a campaign to have every pair of jogging shoes and every track-suit compulsorily marked with the words JOGGING RUINS THE ENVIRONMENT. It could have a bigger following than one might suppose.

Point 3: A doctor writes: 'Half the people you see jogging round the streets today are doing themselves more harm than good.'

Point 4: Gym shoes, once in close contact with dog dirt, never smell quite the same again.

I look forward to hearing Dr Owen's comments in reply but I must warn him that nothing he says will persuade me to join the SDP.

Point 5: My doubts about the SDP increase daily.

Horizontal Jogging

(See Sex, the Middle-Aged Man and.)

Marathon Running

I have no first-hand experience of these increasingly popular events, nor do I wish to. Clearly, those who take part in the London Marathon fall into two quite separate categories: serious athletes who are actually trying to win the thing, and crackpot amateurs who are in it either because they have been sponsored by their local pub with the aim of raising money for charity, or because they are Fleet Street hacks desperate for a story.

I cannot feel that I fit easily into either of these groupings.

From friends who live in Blackheath where the race starts come appalling tales of thousands of grotesque figures dressed in string vests and shorts several sizes too small, clustered around the starting point, their unattractive limbs covered until the last possible moment in converted plastic rubbish bags, relieving themselves *à la francaise* with grim abandon in full view of the gathered multitudes before padding off in the direction of the London Docks and some unaccountable form of personal triumph.

It beats me. But then so, I daresay, would most of them.

(See Dempster, Nigel; Savile, Jimmy; and Fund-Raising, the Middle-Aged Man and.)

Mini-Marathon Running

The sort of thing middle-aged men who normally never take exercise go in for for a bit of a lark and nearly die in the attempt. A friend of mine entered one of these during a local carnival last summer. For most of the seven-mile course, he was paced by a twelve-year-old boy. He was congratulating himself on his unexpected resources of stamina when, a few hundred yards from the finish, the boy said, 'Would you mind if I run a bit faster now? My friends will all be watching and I wouldn't want them to think this is the best I can do.'

Keep-Fit Exercises

Known always in my youth as the Daily Dozen, these have a number of distinct advantages for the middle-aged man over almost all other forms of exercise.

* You don't have to buy special clothing or equipment.
* You are not dependent on the weather.
* You don't have to waste time travelling somewhere to do them.
* You don't have to waste time waiting for others to turn up.
* You don't have to suffer the embarrassment of exposing your ungainly flab and your general inability to perform such simple tasks as touching your knees in front of a lot of people you don't know very well.
* You can perform a lot of different exercises in a fairly short space of time.
* You can start and stop when you feel like it.
* You rarely need to exercise for more than ten minutes a day to achieve the full benefit.
* You can listen to the *Today* programme at the same time, and if you are a tycoon with a remote-control telephone, you can even dictate breathless letters to your secretary in the office.

There are also certain built-in disadvantages:

* Unless you are very single-minded, the temptation to give up after about a minute and a half is often overwhelming.
* There is always a danger the children might burst in on you while you are in the middle of failing to pull off a Sitting Toe Touch, as a result of which your powers of parental authority could be seriously affected for years to come.
* Without expert supervision you could easily do yourself a nasty injury. A friend of mine pulled a muscle in his back while trying his first Trunk Rotation and still hasn't quite recovered three years later.
* Close contact with the Wilton during press-ups can leave you sneezing and snuffling for the rest of the day.
* While lying on your back doing your Leg Raises, your attention will inevitably be directed with unusual concentration towards parts of the room which under normal circumstances pass un-observed. It will be only a matter of time before you have convinced yourself that (a) your wife/daily is falling short with the dusting and (b) the ceiling, and very probably the entire room, is in drastic need of redecoration.
* You feel so stiff and sore the morning following your first session that it is at least a week before you feel up to continuing, by which stage any possible benefit you might be on the point of gaining has gone and you have to start all over again.
* It is as extraordinarily lonely and boring an occupation as it would be possible for anyone to devise.

Attempts, successful by all accounts, to inject a little fun into one's Daily Dozen have been introduced by record companies. Gone are the days when Eileen Fowler would bark orders at you to the sound of a heavy-handed piano accompaniment. Nowadays, bedrooms and sitting rooms up and down the country are jumping to the sounds of Diana Ross telling the nation's great unfit to 'Work That Body' and Felicity Kendal encouraging them to 'Shape Up and Dance'.

Men who have long nurtured fantasies of being disciplined by Angela Rippon can realise their wildest dreams now that she, too, has lent her brisk, no-nonsense accents to a record called 'Shape Up and Dance, Volume Two'. At the latest count, the Rippon instructions ('Stretch, two, three, four . . . Push, two, three, four' etc.) to the accompaniment of such oddly inapt titles as 'It's a Love Thing' and 'Land of Make Believe', have been introduced into over one hundred thousand homes up and down the land.

Any day now I daresay we shall be treated to the sound of Ludovic Kennedy urging us along on our rowing machines to the strains of 'The Eton Boating Song', and Magnus Magnusson instructing us in chair-bound callisthenics, backed by the Old Norse Music Society's rendering of the *Saga of Thor*.

I have always been struck by the fact that so many of today's Keep Fit courses have been devised by members of Her Majesty's Armed Forces. While I can see that the exercises devised for ITV and the *Sunday Times* by Captain Simon Cook and Sergeant Tony Toms of the Royal Marine Commandos might well prove invaluable should one ever be called upon to scale Beachy Head or run across the Scottish Highlands carrying a knapsack filled with hunks of granite, I have never quite understood why the Royal Canadian Air Force should feel themselves uniquely qualified to instruct the average town dweller in physical fitness. The occasions upon which one is likely to be called upon to perform 'Back lying, legs straight, feet together, hands clasped behind head. Sit up and raise legs in bent position, at the same time twist to touch right elbow to left knee' while at the controls of a modern jet fighter are surely few and far between. I can only suppose that aircrews in Canada have so little to do, they have to think of some way to pass the time. I dread to think what the Swiss might come up with, given half a chance.

A friend of mine who kindly lent me his ancient, yellowing copy of the Canadian Air Force exercises admitted ruefully that he had never in a dozen years succeeded in getting past the first two pages. I can't say I'm all that surprised. I was so exhausted after ploughing through the long and elaborate explanation of the 5 BX plan for men that when it came to the section headed 'How to Begin', I had to lie down and rest for half an hour.

Altogether more enjoyable and beneficial (especially for the arms and throat muscles) are the Breton Fishermen's Exercises. (See diagram overleaf.)

Health Clubs

In my youth these were known as gyms. As a schoolboy I spent many an unhappy hour with my nose against a dusty floor trying to keep a straight back during press-ups or standing in a line nervously waiting my turn to run forward and vault over – or in my case through – a wooden horse.

As I understood it in those days, only two sorts of adults frequented gyms: professional bruisers in leather helmets and jockstraps who punched bags and skipped about snorting through their noses and planning bank robberies, and conscientious actors who did a week or two's weight-lifting in order to 'get into shape' for a particularly punishing role.

I couldn't see that these sort of places had anything to offer an intellectual like myself. Even when a stunt man in a TV commercial I wrote offered us all free goes in a gym he'd opened somewhere near Marylebone High Street, images of dirty wallbars and sweat-stained track-suits lurched into my mind and I declined his kind offer.

And then one day, gyms became health clubs, and all the smart people started going to them.

I, however, remained very much a Doubting Thomas. As far as exercising my increasingly flabby muscles on rowing machines and stationary bicycles went, my attitude remained very much the same as at school when I had watched all my friends marching up amid thunderous applause to collect their school colours for some sport or other – envious but unwilling.

Re the massaging sessions which one gathered were all the rage among desk-bound executives and were said to relax, stimulate and increase potency and willpower all at the same time, I was under no illusions whatever. Supposing these to be soothing, gentle affairs, I had once been unwise enough to order a massage from a large Levantine-looking fellow in the Turkish Baths in Jermyn Street – now, alas, defunct (the baths not the masseur) – only to discover that when the fellow was finally able to locate any muscular tissue embedded deep in the fat, he treated it with such ferocious contempt that I was barely able to move for at least a week afterwards.

I was rather more reassured by the club to which a friend of mine invited me for lunch a year or two ago. 'It's in St James's,' he told me. 'You can't miss it.' He being a man of some worldly success, I visualised White's and was rather taken aback, on descending a staircase, to find myself in a small and obviously select health club, where, after a strenuous go on the weights and the bicycle and a vigorous session on the massage table, businessmen on the fringes of middle age would then sit about in towelling dressing gowns drinking fresh orange juice and picking at salads and discussing their latest deals.

I wondered if this companionable method of body maintenance

might be rather my style, until I was told the annual subscription. I can only suppose the sort of members they had there claimed it against tax, as a necessary business expense. 'To public relations . . .', 'To entertaining foreign clients . . .' – that sort of thing.

I was rather more taken with the facilities offered by the Royal Automobile Club in Pall Mall to which the ex-editor of the *Sunday Times* once invited me for a quick trouncing at squash (me, not him), followed by fifty punishing lengths of the pool, (him, not me), drinks in the bar and a further week of immobility. This was an altogether more suitable place to invite influential contacts – publishers, politicians, newspaper editors etc. – for discreet *tête-à-têtes* over a chop and a bottle of claret. I could see the entry in my Diaries: 'Lunched at the RAC with David English after an excellent game of squash. His backhand is coming along very promisingly. We talked of the latest developments at North-cliffe House and he sounded me out on possible contenders for the job of Men's Fashion Editor. Reading between the lines, I have a feeling he'd like me to take it on, but said nothing. The claret there is really first class.'

On reflection I am rather relieved that I did not in fact have my name put forward for membership since (a) I cannot think of a single inflential person I actually wish to lunch with, (b) I am so fed up at being beaten at squash by everyone I know that I have finally hung up my racket once and for all, (c) I hate swimming, (d) it costs £300 to join and (e) lots of exciting places have sprung up in recent years offering a far wider range of health-giving facilities that the RAC could ever hope to do.

All right, so I may not feel an urgent need for Ear Piercing, Reflexology, Waxing, or Nail Sculpture, but the prospect of Nautilus Gym, Jacuzzi, Aerobics, Callisthenics, California Workout and Yoga at Body's in the King's Road, with James Hunt's ex-girlfriend is, for a middle-aged flabby on the lookout for a new lease of life in every sense, intriguing to say the least.

I was even tempted at one time to enrol in one of these dance studios in Covent Garden that one hears are all the rage. As winner of the Twist Competition at the Brancaster Staithe Sailing Club Dance in 1960, runner-up in a major Madison contest in the ski resort of Hochsoelden in January 1962, and an erstwhile exponent of the quickstep *sans pareil* in North Norfolk, I do not doubt that my natural exuberance and sense of rhythm would be more than welcome. On the other hand if, as I strongly suspect, it's all noisy reggae music and sweat-stained leotards and angry left-wing housewives from Kentish Town without any make-up, then I feel I'd be wiser to remember my great dancing days as they were rather than to attempt a foolish comeback.

For a while I withheld my judgement. And then one day I was chatting with a friend and happened to mention the problem I was experiencing in finding a single pair of trousers that I could do up without breathing in very hard first.

He said he knew exactly how I felt; he'd had the same trouble himself. However, since attending the Westside International Health Centre in Kensington twice a week for a 'workout', he had not only made a lot of new friends and discovered that inside his old flabby frame was a hard, lean, muscular body that was the envy of many a fellow half his age, but he now made it his business to broadcast the message of *mens sana in corpore sano* loudly and clearly to whoever was prepared to listen to it.

He then proceeded to trot out a whole lot of stuff about noradrenaline, the dangers of heart disease etc., adding that it was a well-known fact that the fitter a man is, the more sexually attractive to women, and that, since taking up regular exercise, he had felt and performed like 'a thoroughbred stallion'.

He certainly could have fooled me – and, I would have thought, most women.

Personally, I have never felt myself to be a less amusing dinner or theatre companion for want of a well-shaped pectoral or a bulging bicep. On the other hand, there are those of my age group who are convinced that being in tip-top physical condition is a *sine qua non* for a successful career and that stamina on the exercise bicycle equals stamina in bed, and it was on their behalf rather than for any personal advancement that I decided to submit Westside to the Matthew Value-for-Money Test.

My first impression was of a friendly, easygoing atmosphere. If the signed photographs of film and TV celebrities like John Curry, Timothy West, Valerie Singleton and Patrick McNee were any indication of the sort of people one could expect to be rubbing shoulders with, then the £200 a year membership fee was certainly worth every penny. I must admit, I had never really thought of Terry Wogan as a serious press-up-man, but then of course he is very young-looking for his age.

Taking everything into account, I decided not to put my name up for membership there and then but to go instead for a single afternoon of gym, sun-bed and massage to see how I got on.

Over a 'taste-tingling' health juice in Dr Banana's Jungle-Fun

Bar, I met my instructor, an irritatingly well-built young man with, to my mind, rather over-developed shoulders.

I didn't altogether care for the rather critical way he looked me up and down. I tried to point out that, as a writer, one cannot avoid a certain amount of sitting and bending forward, hence the slight thickening of the waist. He replied that that was not really a valid excuse and that everyone is capable of keeping himself in trim whatever his profession. It's all a matter of self-respect.

He then led the way through to the gymnasium, a large, brightly-lit, mirrored room, full of elaborate weight-lifting machines, one of which was being operated with enviable ease by a deadpan man-mountain.

Despite my live-again fitness-fanatic friend's assurances that 'Tasty young birds like nothing better than to run their fingers over a *belle musculataire*, but that doesn't mean to say they want a gorilla on their hands', I was sufficiently inspired by this incredible hulk's performance on the lateral pull-downs to want to start pumping iron myself without more ado. I was quite disappointed when my instructor informed me that he would be starting me off on the beginner's circuit.

All right, one hears of comparatively young men dropping dead from too much sudden exertion, but surely, stepping up and down a wooden box a few times was taking caution a little tto far.

I must admit, one or two of the exercises taxed me more than most, especially the fifteen Sit-Ups and Twists. Needless to say my instructor made it all look absurdly easy, but then would he look so clever, faced with a blank sheet of paper and a typewriter?

One of the things that irritates me about fitness fanatics is their competitiveness. I suppose the fact is that some people feel they need to prove something by pushing themselves to the limit, but personally, I know when enough's enough. My instructor could scarcely contain his disgust when I told him that I was pushed for time (no joke intended) and wanted to cut short the circuit in favour of a sun-bed session. Well, I was sorry to deprive him of the satisfaction of seeing a well-known public figure making a fool of himself, but I couldn't help that. The whole essence of physical fitness is, after all, matter over mind and at that moment mine was in no mind to argue the toss.

There were two beds in the sun-room, and even though I was alone, I took great care to keep a towel round my middle when I lay down. There's no knowing what these powerful rays can do to you. I also kept my eyes tightly closed despite the fact that I was wearing goggles.

Even so, at the end of the session half an hour later, I found I was quite unable to see a thing. As a result, I stumbled around the room for quite a long while before going hard into the washbasin in the corner. I was convinced I had gone blind until I remembered I had forgotten to take off the goggles.

After that, I made my way upstairs for a massage, feeling unusually trim and full of healthy sunshine. I had not realised it was possible to acquire a real tan after only one session and was admiring myself in the large changing-room mirror when I suddenly realised that it wasn't a mirror at all but an open door and that I was walking towards a particularly muscular foreign type coming from the showers.

My Egyptian masseur, Hysam, was first rate. The idea of massaging towards the heart and thus stimulating circulation had never occurred to me before. At all events, I felt so fit when I finally left that I ran the length of Kensington High Street, skipping light as a young ram and swinging on all the lamp-posts like Gene Kelly.

It made me wonder if there might not be something to my friend's sex appeal theory after all. I don't think I have ever had quite so many looks from women in my life.

It was only when I got home that I discovered all my fly buttons were undone, but I really don't think that can have had anything to do with it.

Exercise Equipment

I have long pondered the possibility of leavening the appalling drudgery of daily keep-fit exercises (when I remember to do them, that is) with the added zest of gadgetry. It wasn't just the thought that the very fact of having oars to pull or pedals to push must be marginally more interesting than heaving oneself up and down against the broadloom or lying on one's back waving one's feet in the air that set me thinking along these lines, so much as the feeling that, by laying out good money on a rowing machine or an exercise bicycle, one would at least be duty bound to derive as much value for one's initial outlay as possible.

Which, though, would be the ideal machine for me, given that I have neither the room nor the wallet for more than one?

As an ex-Oxford University oarsman, the sensation of swinging with my body between my knees would certainly present fewer difficulties to me than to most. Well, when I say university oarsman, I was picked to train for a week with the squad of freshmen by the President of the OUBC as part of a drive to halt the sudden, inexplicable run of successes being enjoyed by Cambridge in the early sixties. One of my fellow wet-bobs was Crown Prince Harald of Norway. We often enjoyed a joke together, and on one memorable occasion he took my towel in mistake for his. Or rather, vice-versa. I daresay a lot of opportunist types would have said nothing and hung on to the royal material and had it framed and hung on the wall as a conversation piece; but, of course, as anyone who has ever rowed in an eight knows, trust is the very foundation of a good crew, and I made a point of returning it the following day. It was a pity he had to go and lose mine, but these things happen. Curiously enough, I happened to be in Trafalgar Square a year or two ago when his very charming wife, Princess Sonja, performed the lighting-up ceremony of the Christmas tree. Had I not been in a bit of a rush to get home, I might well have made myself known to her.

I can't remember now why I decided not to continue with the training. I'm not saying I would automatically have made it into the Blue Boat, but somehow I cannot imagine that the President would have invested all the time and energy in me that he did, had he not seen me as a serious contender for a place.

Still, I think it was generously agreed that I made a not inconsiderable contribution to my college Novice Eight, and the fact that we did not make it past the second leg in the Novice Regatta I put down to indifferent coxing. All mouth and no action, as we say in rowing circles. In fact, there came a moment when I was convinced that if I heard that voice screeching at me about my follow-through once again, I would kill its beastly owner with my oar.

Indeed, I feel sure that it is the memory of that fellow's endlessly demanding tones that finally persuaded me that, whatever type of exercising machine I finally ended up with, it was never going to be a rowing machine.

A bicycle, on the other hand, would, I decided, bring back nothing but happy memories of my childhood days in Surrey – of long summer afternoons spent pedalling through the shady woods, my aertex shirt sticking to my skin with the effort and my grey shorts well nigh worn out by the Brookes saddle . . .

That was until I discovered (a) how much a really good, top-of-the-range machine costs, (b) how much it weighs, (c) what a very nasty smell it makes when you start applying the brake to increase the pressure, and (d) that to use it properly involves such a complicated series of procedures, from taking your temperature at given moments, to looking up log tables in order to work out your precise effort and work rate, that the average owner would need to take degrees in medicine and higher mathematics before actually daring to mount the thing.

And then one day I was thumbing through the *Daily Mail* when my eye was caught by the dramatic words 'Powercharge your body with the Bullworker Super X 5'. If the subsequent copy was to be believed, the Bullworker people had 'doubled – yes, doubled – the dynamic limit of the early models – a 100 per cent increase in the power range'.

This was exciting news for anyone, like myself, keen to tune himself up physically – especially as one could try it out for fourteen days for nothing. All it would take, apparently, was five minutes of my time per day, and if I was not 'delighted with the *measurable* increase' in my strength and the 'all too *visible* improvement' in my appearance, I could return it and get my money back.

In fact, this very simple deal was rather more complicated than it first appeared, since, by the time I set off on my holiday to Suffolk, the thing hadn't arrived.

When I rang the Bullworker people in Norwich to explain, they pointed out that the free fourteen-day trial period began from the moment it arrived in my home. The solution was simple. I rang the daily, who had very kindly said she would forward all our mail, to say that, if a long parcel arrived from Norwich, would she be very kind and refuse to accept it, in which case the postman would take it away and store it at the local sorting office whence I would collect it on my return.

Obviously I didn't make myself clear, because a few days later the Bullworker arrived, duly re-addressed, at my holiday home.

Now then – did this mean that the fourteen-day trial began from the moment it was delivered to my home in London, or from the time I actually received it? If the former, then I had already lost up to four days' worth while the parcel chuntered around south-east England. And to judge by the struggle it took me just to undo the box the Bullworker came in, I needed every second of body-building I could get. I rang Norwich to clarify the situation only to find that the line to London was on the blink.

Fortunately, I am not a man to allow a small setback like that to interfere with the major task in hand and I determined to waste no more time.

The blond, muscular, obviously Teutonic young man pictured on the wall-chart demonstrating the various exercises appeared to be wearing, in addition to an unnecessary abundance of chest hair and a maddeningly smug grin, a pair of what I can only describe as long underpants. If there was some technical benefit to be gained from dressing in this eccentric fashion, then I was just going to have to go without it. £28.40 seemed to me quite enough to lay out for the doubtful advantage of well-defined abdominals, without adding to the cost with comic clothing. If the device couldn't turn flab into muscle equally well under a shirt and grey flannel trousers, then I wanted nothing to do with it.

The chart suggested six reasonably undemanding exercises which one should try for the first five days before moving on to anything more strenuous. 'The key to success,' it declared, 'is to start out slowly.' There was even a little place provided for writing in one's daily Muscleometer readings.

Despite a slight trembling of the legs that invariably seemed to result from Exercise 3 (but then how often is one called upon to sit upright in a chair with your legs stuck straight out in front of you and a Bullworker waving about on your ankles?), I was gratified to discover that I was able to perform all the exercises without the slightest difficulty. I only wish I could truthfully say that I felt any the better for it.

According to the free booklet, 'After about four to five work-outs, most men experience an exhilarating sensation of renewed fitness that is a real turn-on; muscles springing back to life, a powerful charge of energy coursing through your veins making you feel stronger, dynamic, raring to go, one hundred per cent alive again.'

That's as may be, but then I daresay most men are not unfortunate enough to suffer the painful experience I did on Day 5 – viz: sitting on the edge of a chair with one end of the Bullworker resting on one knee and pulling down on the outer ropes as per Exercise 4, when the stupid thing takes it into its head to come whanging backwards with great force, catching one a direct bullseye in the orchestras, thus putting one completely *hors de combat* for at least a week.

I did ring Norwich with my carefully rehearsed joke about 'not so much a Bullworker – more a Ballworker' and a sharp enquiry as to how they wished to have it returned, only to realise that, what with one thing and another, I had overrun my free trial period and was landed with the device whether I wanted it or not.

To add to my irritation, I now learn from a physical fitness expert of my acquaintance that all these gadgets are quite unnecessary and all a chap of my age need to do to keep himself from total atrophy is make sure he gets out of breath once a day. Hardly reassuring advice for one who does that every time he gets up out of a chair.

Still, at least that way I need have no fears for my manhood.

Sports and Games

Middle age is the time when huge numbers of men suddenly decide to relive their youth by taking up various games which (a) they never played in their youth at all or (b) if they did, they were extremely bad at and spent much of their time trying to get out of. Viz:

Football

By which I mean soccer. Happily I am excused this one, since an essential prerequisite for the middle-aged man is that he should be blessed with soccer-mad sons for whose benefit his interest in actually playing the game is initially rekindled. This usually takes the form of putting on a track-suit and kicking a plastic ball around with them and their chums in the park on a Sunday morning. Before they know what, scratch games have been got up with other well-intentioned fathers and suddenly they are into a regular weekly fixture situation from which it is impossible to extricate themselves for years to come – even though the boys themselves may long since have moved on to better things. At the time of writing, my sons are aged two and a half and four months and the name of Glen Hoddle is still, I am delighted to say, as unknown to them as Adam Ant. It is my intention that things should remain that way until I am way past soccer-playing age – although, to my horror, I actually caught myself, only the other day, returning a ball that my elder son had quite arbitrarily kicked in my direction. I must watch myself.

Rugger

Should only be played by over-thirty-five-year-olds who (a) suddenly acquire an inordinate taste for beer, bawdy songs and the tang of embrocation and (b) who have known what it is to find themselves under 200 stone of bloodthirsty scrum. And probably not even then.

Cricket

It is a little-known fact that I once played cricket for England. Third Test against Corfu, 1975. In Corfu Town. I scored four hard-earned runs (you would appreciate how hard if you have drunk as many ouzos as I had at lunchtime, had to take guard with a bat borrowed from an ex-captain of Somerset which was so heavy I rarely managed to lift it before the ball was in the wicket-keeper's hands, and if you have ever faced bowling on a coconut matting beneath which lurk strategically-placed pebbles, the location of which is known only to the opposing team).

I also bowled two rather expensive overs for which I was heartily congratulated by my captain who was anxious to make it appear as equal a contest as was humanly possible.

This was the sole occasion on which I have been tempted to take the field since school and, as it turned out, the last. I can quite see the attraction of the weekly village game for the middle-aged player – good company, pleasant surroundings, some not too strenuous exercise, clothing that actually enhances the appearance, egg sandwiches and home-made jam sponge for tea, and a general feeling that one is enjoying English life at its very best. Like David Sheppard, however, I believe in going out at the top. I cannot believe that my country's call will come again, and if I cannot play cricket for England, then I'd prefer not to play it at all.

Tennis

An increasingly popular sport amongst the middle-aged, readers of the *Guardian* and members of the SDP – thanks to some admirable PR work on the part of Messrs Peter Ustinov, Roy Jenkins, Milton Shulman, J. Drobny *et al.* If a man like Reginald Bosanquet can get through three sets without suffering a cardiac arrest, anyone can.

Although most of today's *aficionados* favour the track-suit, the game does nevertheless afford certain middle-aged players the opportunity to wheel their old school cricketing flannels out of mothballs, thread a rolled-up school 1st XI silk square through the belt loops and spring about athletically like Jean Borotra. Eccentric behaviour of this sort is best confined to private tennis parties in friends' gardens if one does not wish to run the very real risk of catcalls and shouts of 'Go it, Suzanne Lenglen!'

It is also advisable not to go near a tennis court for at least a day after watching Wimbledon on television. The temptation to emulate the Tanner serve and the Connors double-backhand cross-court return can all too often end in disaster.

Some basic skill is also desirable – e.g. being able to return the occasional service and/or return. Games which consist of one-stroke rallies or less are rarely satisfying, as I would be the first to confirm.

Squash

A friend of mine died of a heart attack on a squash court at the age of thirty-four. I die a death every time I try to play, too. This is because (a) I am one of those completely untutored players who believe that all you have to do is rush about smashing the ball as and when the opportunity arises and generally getting up a good sweat and (b) I invariably find myself playing against men who know better and merely stand in the middle of the court cool and relaxed to the end, lobbing the ball wherever they fancy while I scuttle around them from one side of the court to the other turning an increasingly violent shade of red and giving myself a dose of stress that makes an hour in a traffic jam on the M4 seem like a week's holiday at La Réserve Beaulieu.

Bearing in mind that my late friend played soccer and cricket the Oxford University in his day and was a first-class all-round sportsman, incompetent middle-aged players should consider either playing only against people of their own low standard or giving up. Preferably the latter.

Swimming

Another form of exercise strongly favoured by the middle-aged man without any background of sporting excellence to his credit.

About a year ago, in a fit of unwonted enthusiasm, I took out a subscription for three months for the swimming pool at Dolphin Square, Pimlico.

Having anticipated a lively, youthful atmosphere (chaps doing honey-pots off the top board, pretty girls in bikinis splashing each other etc.) it came as a grave disappointment to be confronted by a poolful of silent, grim-faced individuals in bathing caps and goggles, looking like a bunch of mutants from outer space, ploughing relentlessly from one end to the other in a slow, almost sub-aquatic crawl. In the circumstances, I felt that my bouncy, head-up breast-stroke would be so out of place as to cause offence, and possibly even expulsion. Fortunately, I have always been a good mimic and I was soon powering my way through the chlorine with the best of them.

What I had not taken into account, however, was (a) that if you swim half submerged, your nose keeps filling up with water, (b) unless you keep your eyes wide open (and thus in a permanent state of agony), you keep bumping into other swimmers, and possibly the end wall, and (c) turning your head to one side every now and then in order to take a quick breath is far more difficult than Johnny Weissmuller ever made it look. (Mark you, everything that Johnny Weissmuller ever did is more difficult than it looks.)

The main problem is disposing of the previous mouthful of air before taking on board a fresh one. In the absence of any expert advice, I decided the only possible solution was to blow it out into the water first, thus making the way ahead even more obscure than before.

The answer to all my problems clearly lay in a pair of goggles and a pink plastic nose clip. Perhaps I have an unusually shaped face, I don't know. All I can tell you is that the water still managed to get in behind the goggles. I tried tightening them, but merely succeeded in giving myself a headache. As for the nose clip, this kept slipping off with such monotonous regularity that I was finally reduced to a sort of *unijambiste* version of the trudgeon as I struggled to stop the wretched thing floating, like a discarded piece of sexual paraphernalia, to the bottom of the pool.

The answer, I suppose, is that some of us have developed further away from the marine creatures of pre-history than others.

Golf

At best, as enjoyable a form of character building, mental concentration and achievement of potential as the middle-aged man is likely to find anywhere; at worst, a long walk punctuated by eighteen disaapointments – a terrible cliché for which I make absolutely no apology whatever, since everything about golf is a cliché, from cruel jokes about the golf freak pausing before a putt on the eleventh to raise his hat at a passing funeral ('Must show respect to the wife, you know'), to real-life shockers about golf widows.

Of all games taken up by the middle-aged none is more compulsive and potentially all-consuming than golf. Just one well-struck shot in a whole round is enough to ensure that you will be out there on the first tee again at the earliest possible opportunity.

It can also be extremely expensive – especially if, like a neighbour of my father's, you suddenly convince yourself at the age of fifty that the reason you have not managed to get your handicap below twenty, despite playing three or four times every weekend of your life, is simply that you are naturally left-handed. And when, having sold your old clubs, bought your set of left-handed clubs and paid for several months' worth of left-handed lessons, you then realise that you were quite wrong and that you simply must reverse the entire process immediately if you want to be ready in time for the Spring Foursomes, then do not be too surprised if you find you have to remove the children from public school and give up expensive luxuries like heating, clothes and food.

As a topic of conversation, a shot-by-shot account of a round of golf achieves an interest-rating with non-golfers on about the same level as the synopsis of the latest Dick Francis thriller would with the Dalai Lama.

But this is all dull negative stuff. Away with melancholy and on with the, if not motley, then at least the Lee Trevino golfing shoes, the Fuzzy Zoeller West of Scotland lambswool pullover, the Brian Barnes lightweight, non-slip golfing glove, the Johnny Miller slimline, yellow and aquamarine check slacks and the Raymond Floyd cumfifit, anti-rupture athletic support, out with the American Express card and into the half-hour queue waiting to drive off on the first tee of any golf course you care to choose within a radius of fifty miles of London.

What better way for the senior advertising executive to consolidate a million pounds' worth of business than by allowing a client to win by three and two over the West Course at Wentworth – preferably accompanied by Bernard Gallagher, the club professional?

What more pleasant way for the actor on the provincial tour of *Equus* to pass those long afternoons in Norwich and Leeds and Southsea than by packing his clubs and taking out temporary membership at the local golf club? Who knows – it could be only a matter of time before his name comes to the attention of whoever it is who organises those Celebrity Pro-Am golf series on BBC2, and before he knows what, he is up there at Gleneagles Hotel, all expenses paid, knocking round the Queen's Course with the likes of Lee Trevino, Ben Crenshaw, Bruce Forsyth and Telly Savalas, winning himself Waterford crystal by the armful and assuring himself of a place among the all-time greats of showbusiness and a warm, personal friendship with Bob Hope himself . . .

There you are, you see. Golf is just one big cliché. Like middle age.

Skiing

Aside from bullfighting, Thai Boxing and Motorcycle Scrambling, probably the closest the middle-aged man is likely to come to understanding what Hemingway was on about. The sheer knee-trembling terror that is naturally built into any activity as unnatural as strapping a pair of planks to the bottom of your feet and sliding downhill cannot fail to appeal to the man who has reached the age of forty without once having been afforded the opportunity to test himself against a charging rhino, on a 900 cc Yamaha round the TT circuit on the Isle of Man, or alone in the back streets of Manchester's Moss-Side on a hot Saturday night in June.

Those of us who learnt to ski in the fifties with our feet rigidly clamped onto skis that stood two feet or more above our heads, our knees locked into excruciating snowplough positions, being commanded by granite-faced Austrians to 'bend zer knees', and cheered on by the prospect of nothing more relaxing than an hour's strenuous quickstepping in our ski boots at teatime followed by an evening of catching greasy pigs and having our bottoms smacked by sweating herdsmen in tight leather shorts, may be excused for the somewhat superior attitude we adopt towards our debutant contemporaries.

The short skis on which so many are taught nowadays, the ski-lifts conveniently placed outside the door of the custom-built hotel, the instructors with their well-developed command of English, all help to make life easier for the beginner. But is that really what skiing is all about? Can today's skier, for all his facile skills and expensive ski-suits and undoubted expertise on the discotheque floor, really call himself a man of the mountains?

But there you are. That's only me being boring and middle-aged again, as usual.

Sailing

Possibly the ultimate in middle-aged sporting activities, it combines all the qualities that only the truly middle-aged can draw upon easily and without question: the ability to command; the desire to get away from wife, family and responsibilities and be alone for a while; the urge for physical activity; the need to feel at one with the elements and thus to achieve a sense of self-awareness unattainable on the Piccadilly Line at 8.30 on a Monday morning; the ability to spend money – not wisely perhaps, bearing in mind the mortgage and the school fees, but well.

The urge for exploration lies never very deep beneath the skin of many a man, who in the middle of his life looks at his worldly achievements and tells himself that there must be more to it all than a full appointments diary and the office pension scheme.

Nor, for much the same reasons, does the urge to relive the childhood he never knew. The man who builds elaborate sand-castles on the beach does so not because it gives his children pleasure (indeed, like him at that age, they stand around and watch only out of a natural sense of loyalty) but because it pleases *him*.

In the same way, the reason I was so determined to buy a small sailing dinghy when I moved to a small seaside town in Suffolk a year or two ago was not, as I told myself at the time, that when I was a boy on holiday on the North Norfolk coast I used to spend every waking hour sailing in and out of the salt water creeks, but because I never did anything of the sort.

Nor was I content with some fibreglass number that was light and practical and easy to maintain. Oh no. It had to be clinker-built and chunky with a single red sail, just like the ones in *Swallows and Amazons*.

(Incidentally, it just goes to show how middle-aged I am that I should nurture such romantic memories of Arthur Ransome's stories. Parents nowadays would think twice about letting a bunch of young kids set off alone in a heavy old dinghy, for days on end, without life jackets. Quite apart from the risks of drowning, gippy tummy from inadequately prepared camp food, exposure and adder bites, anyone who would allow their children to come within a hundred miles of a weirdo calling himself Captain Flint, who lives alone on a houseboat with a parrot, is asking for trouble.)

Vaguely at the back of my mind was the idea that one day I would teach my boys to sail in *Sand Martin*, as I quaintly named my little craft. Of course, I realise now, having ricked my back a dozen times trying to heave the wretched thing out of the water, that the whole thing is quite impracticable and that if a fully grown man risks injury every time he tries to launch it, then the chances of two small boys even being able to wheel it to the slipway are pretty remote. When it comes to the point, I shall have to sell the old hulk and replace it with what I should have bought in the first place – a fibreglass number that is light and practical and easy to maintain.

I had fondly supposed also that one day I would move up to an ocean-going vessel with a cabin and bunk beds and perhaps even a small radar set to help get me across to Dieppe for a shopping spree or to the Brittany coast for whatever reason it is that people sail to the Brittany coast. This supposition has less to do with a marked reluctance among my family and friends to join me on my little expeditions up the Snape or down to Orford (although I must say the next person who on seeing my boat for the first time exclaims, 'Oh, it's not quite as big as I'd imagined' can expect to feel the rough side of my tongue) than with a vague feeling that onward and upward should be the keynote of a happy and successful life.

The fact is, though, that you're either born a small-boat man or you're not, and frankly I have yet to be persuaded that the flap of the genoa and the flicker of the radar is really for me. Allow a middle-aged man to get his teeth into anything over a dozen feet long and there's no knowing what deep water he may not get himself into. Bernard Moitessier, Donald Crowhurst, Edward Heath. Need I say more?

In which I undertake a crash course in yoga
and diets of varying degrees of
unpleasantness, describe my experiences at
two well-known health hydros, nearly
interview Ava Gardner, and explain why I
could never become a health food fanatic.

Chapter Four

If I seem to have come to no definite conclusion regarding the need or desirability of sport or indeed exercise of any kind as a help towards surviving middle age, it is because I am in two minds about it myself.

Having been brought up in true public-school style, with sufficient expertise to turn my hand to most sports, should circumstances demand it, I derive great pleasure from the occasional game of croquet and the odd hour spent ambling through the Surrey countryside on a docile hack. I am also, after nearly twenty-five years, still keen enough on skiing to work on my carved turns and deep powder action once a year with all the enthusiasm of a beginner.

However, when it comes to prolonged bouts of intense physical activity of the sort required for squash, work-outs in gymnasia etc., I harbour the strongest possible doubts.

I remember once enquiring of my friend Daniel Topolski, the distinguished oarsman and coach of the continuously successful Oxford University Boat Race crew, what it feels like to be approaching forty and still as fit as a man half his age. The enquiry was, I must admit, motivated by sheer envy.

He replied that he never really thought about it, but that when he did, it was to remind himself that anyone who achieves a very high degree of physical fitness must expect to have to maintain it for the rest of his life if he does not wish to run the risk of heart failure.

This merely confirmed me in my suspicion that the one great drawback to exercise for adults is that, once taken up it has to be kept up, and frankly I have enough trouble with my waistline as it is without the added anxiety of collapsing pectorals. As the saying goes in rugby club bars, 'Old rugger players never die; they only look that way.'

Osbert Sitwell had the right idea. He held to a theory that games and all forms of violent exercise were totally unnecessary and that a grown man could keep healthy on one sharp twenty-minute walk a day. He would therefore get his chauffeur to drive him to a nearby wood which he would walk through before meeting the car on the other side. An excellent idea in principle but hard to carry out in practice without a chauffeur.

Having said which, there is one form of exercise which, in spite of its unfortunate associations with beards, open-toed sandals, wholefoods and a general preoccupation with the self, is, I suspect, as beneficial for stiff muscles, tired brains and a low sex drive as everyone who has ever tried it says it is. I refer, of course, to . . .

Yoga

Now before I go any further, I should like to make it clear that, apart from Pakistan's unusually successful Test series against England recently, and the undoubted genius of the retired Indian car mechanic in the next street to ours who has got me out of more expensive visits to the local Renault garage than anyone deserves in a whole lifetime of owning second-hand French cars, and the Great India Restaurant in Lower Sloane Street which does the best takeaway Sag Gosht in London, I do not hold a particularly strong brief for the Indians or their way of life.

I have no desire to sit in a mountain fastness contemplating my navel for months on end, nor can I see that the technique of drawing up gallons of water through my nostrils and discharging them through my bottom is likely to stand me in especially good stead at my age – unless of course things should go really badly for me and I have to resort to appearing in some louche sideshow in Caracas.

I cannot seriously bring myself to believe that the Indians, of all people, have discovered the meaning of life. If they had, and all there was to it was sitting cross-legged on the floor for hours on end chanting strange mantras to oneself, how come most of them are running newsagents' shops and small grocery stores?

On the other hand, I have a feeling there may be more to these funny exercises they've thought up than meets the eye.

Unfortunately, my enthusiasm has been dampened on more than one occasion in the past as a result of unhappy experiences at the hands of so-called qualified yoga teachers.

The first time I dipped my toe into the murky waters of Eastern mysticism was when I enrolled in an evening class for budding yoga maniacs in the echoing chill of a local primary school gymnasium. I remember very little about it except that, after spending several minutes lying on our backs with our eyes closed thinking of absolutely nothing, we were invited to sit up in what is known as the lotus position – a curious arrangement of the limbs which in my case more closely resembled a Jerusalem artichoke.

However, I am nothing if not a trier on these sorts of occasions and I was in the process of awarding myself a metaphorical pat on the back at having sat with my legs crossed for a minute on end without rolling over, when a most excruciating pain shot through my left knee. This not only put me off games for the remainder of the session but has, I am convinced, contributed in no small part to my reluctance to attend Morning Prayer – except, of course, at Christmas and Easter. And even then, upon being invited to join the rest of the congregation in prayer, I am obliged to bend forward in a seated position with one hand held against my forehead like a retired brigadier (see God, the Middle-Aged Man and his Relationship with).

Still, I am not a man who is easily deterred once he has set his mind to something, and a year or two later, on a whim, I bought myself a paperback book entitled *Yoga and Health*, written by an Indian who claimed to have overcome a number of childhood illnesses with the help of yoga, including scarlet fever, dysentery, typhus and cholera. Having myself fallen prone to a number of nasty colds that winter, I was keen to learn his secret.

It lay, I was fascinated to discover, in the chapter entitled: 'OUR GREATEST MISTAKE: WE CANNOT BREATHE!'

It seems that the average man sitting in an office uses only a tenth of the capacity of his lungs, as a result of which most of us miss out on the life force of the universe known as prana.

Now the best way to take this mysterious stuff on board is through the nose – don't ask me why – and the trouble is most of us do our breathing through the mouth – hence all those nasty colds that seem to go around with such monotonous regularity. 'If children were taught nose breathing in school,' writes the author Mr Yesudian, 'it would be possible to raise a new, stronger and more intelligent generation!'

Personally, I have been a nasal breather, man and boy, for over forty years, so when it came to trying out some of the more unusual postures suggested in the book – the grasshopper, the cobra, the peacock etc. – I found that the business of getting the whole operation under way with a full yoga inhalation slightly easier than falling off a log. The problems arose when, having got as far as lying face down with nose and forehead touching the floor, placing my fists on the floor beside my thighs, and making a full inhalation, I would then forget what it was I was supposed to be doing next and have to sit up and refer to the book. As a result any lasting benefit I might hitherto have derived from the exercise was completely lost and I had to begin all over again.

I did try placing the book on the floor in such a way that I could refer to it without having to change position, but the trouble with expensive paperbacks is that they have a maddening habit of closing at precisely the wrong moment, as if of their own accord. I sometimes wondered if the intense concentration I was bringing to bear upon the situation hadn't some part to play in the matter.

I think I might have given up all thoughts of a happier and healthier life had I not happened to meet Mr Ballard.

One day last summer Peter, as I have now learned to address him (we yoga people are all very casual), a freelance yoga teacher, invited me to join one of his classes, assuring me that my lack of experience would prove a drawback neither to myself nor to the other members of the group. Also that, as long as I wore loose, comfortable clothes, it would not matter in the least that I did not possess one of those floppy jogging outfits that are all the rage these days at parties and similar social events.

As one for whom keep-fit exercises have rarely occupied more than ten minutes per day at the outside, I was more than a little taken aback to learn that a typical yoga class lasts *two hours*, if you please. Two hours! You could sit through an entire Alan Ayckbourn comedy in two hours. Or fly to Prague. Or drive to Ipswich. A man could fill two hours with a lifetimes' worth of experiences. But a few simple exercises? How *was* I going to put up with the yawning boredom of it?

In the circumstances, I felt it wise to have a few quiet words with Peter first.

I have, since starting to research this book, become fairly used to personal criticism of one sort or another, and you might suppose that having been the butt of countless jokes and jibes at the hands of dentists, doctors, fitness fanatics and goodness knows who else, I have grown immune to insult. Not so. Resigned possibly, but the barbs, however lightheartedly tossed, still bite as deeply as ever.

So, when Peter cast an expert eye over me and announced that he'd like to 'change that upper area – open it out – enlarge the lungs' (i.e. do something about my narrow, hunched shoulders), I actually found myself for the first time discussing their inadequacy in the same mood of enthusiastic objectivity that one might bring to a subject like the price of four-bedroomed houses in SW12 or Frank Muir's bow ties.

In the next few minutes he outlined several of the benefits of yoga: releases you from tiring emotions, stretches and strengthens the muscles, liberates powers of strength, intelligence and will, keeps you regular etc. etc. All very worthwhile advantages in their own different ways, of course, yet none seized my imagination more thoroughly than the possibility, however faint, that, as a result of a few simple exercises, these slim, sloping shoulders about which I have been so self-conscious ever since the age of ten, might be transformed into a pair of square, masculine girders from which any tailor would be proud to hang a length of best West Country wool.

Was it really possible that, at last, for the first time in over thirty years I should be in a position to stroll around in public at the height of summer without the reassuring disguise of a jacket? That this soft, pear-shaped figure would be converted, as if by magic, into a hard wedge? That I should be able to holiday in St Tropez and take off all my clothes without so much as a second thought? And, most important of all, that those haunting words, uttered in a thoughtless moment in front of a PT class by a cruel headmaster ('Shoulders back. Not you, Matthew. You haven't got any.') would be exorcised from my brain once and for all?

'Let's to it,' I cried, and before I knew what, there I was in the yoga room, my shoes and socks cast carelessly to one side, watching my fellow yogas (yogists? yogurts?) warming to the task in hand by bending themselves almost double over ropes attached to wall bars, while Peter moved among them, mixing words of advice and encouragement with casual conversational chitchat: 'That's it Brenda, dear. Rope against the thighs. You must keep your buttocks high. Did you see *Death in Venice* on the telly last night? Lovely costumes, but *what* a dreary story. Well done George . . .'

There were a dozen of us altogether, ranging from the elderly, white-haired Mr Smith, to the lithe, pencil-thin actress Tracy. Several were, I was glad to notice, every bit as middle-aged as myself. I was slightly disappointed not to be allowed to join in with the warm-up exercises, along with the rest. Still, I'm sure Peter knew what he was doing.

It had been my original intention to take you step by step through the exercises that followed in order that anyone interested in following my example and taking up yoga might have some clear mental picture of what is involved. Indeed, in the interests of veracity, I wrote down Peter's instructions word for word.

At the time they seemed to make perfect sense. Yet looking through them now, they read like extracts from the section of a cookery book entitled 'A Dozen Unusual Ways of Preparing Rabbit':

'Lift shoulders towards ceiling so that neck becomes extended. Raise hips towards ceiling. Keep skin of legs cutting into flesh. Now fibres of thigh muscles will stretch upwards and both knees face directly forward. Waist back and open sternum . . .

'Press heelbones firmly into floor and kneecaps into leg and lift. Tuck the tail bone in and the spine should shoot towards ceiling. Straighten lumbar region, then dorsal area comes forward as skin stretches over shoulder blades . . .'

I cannot pretend to possess more than a passing knowledge of human anatomy, but within moments of the class getting under way it became perfectly obvious to me that 90 per cent of the movements suggested were physically out of the question to all but the most skilful professional contortionists. And yet, the extraordinary thing is that Peter, with his soft, insistent voice constantly urging one on, his eyes always on the move for signs of tiredness, his hands endlessly touching and feeling backs and shoulders, checking through the warmth of the skin for any possible danger signs, somehow not only made one feel one could achieve some diabolical position, but actually lured every member of the class into doing so.

Just listen to this for wishful thinking:

'Now then my dears, sitting on the floor, buttocks level. Stretch heels forward, raise chest and spine, bring heel into groin, keeping the back of the other leg straight and flat on the floor.

Now grab left foot with right hand. Slowly go down until chest takes spine to thigh. Bring the crown of the head forward, working the right side against the strength of the left leg. The front of the chest must work equally with the back. Now move right leg to one side and backwards and hold the right foot with the left hand. Hollow the back, bend forward and work down with the right buttock as we surrender to the spine. Now hold both feet with both hands, work the kneecaps into the legs, sternum first, head last and come up when you have had enough.'

I say no more, except to add that during one particularly complicated movement Tracy actually lay there, back bent double, reading a book on yoga *and laughing*. Secondly, to recommend that nobody actually follows the above instructions without first taking out substantial life insurance, just on the off-chance that I may accidentally have run two or more exercises together. And thirdly to remind you that it went on like this for *two hours*. Can you wonder that I was like a damp dishcloth by the end? And I was only observing. Even the rest period, which was the only part of the proceedings I felt up to joining, took it out of me in no uncertain terms.

And yet, surprising as it may seem there were moments when, by listening to the body's intelligence, I was convinced that my brain became quite detached from humdrum reality. I transcended the mundane and joined all the great yoga masters in realising that what we call life is not reality but illusion.

It is rare moments like these that make the middle-aged man feel that it might be worth going on after all.

Diets

A subject which has spawned more best-selling books in recent years even than the brilliant career of the Princess of Wales, and one which I therefore plan to dispose of without further ado.

Since there appear to be as many diets as people who invent them (or indeed go on them), I shall restrict such observations as I have to make to two – the only two, as it happens, that I have ever personally undertaken. (I recently very nearly allowed a friend to talk me into the famous F-plan diet, on the grounds that it allows one to tuck into all the sort of food one likes best – baked beans, pasta, sweetcorn, bananas, bran flakes . . . I'm not surprised he lost weight. All that fibre must move so fast it doesn't have a chance to do any harm before it's out again. In the end, though, it was the wind that put me off. Some people may think nothing of moving about in polite society while constantly emitting a sound like tearing calico. I do, as it happens.)

The first was the famous grapefruit diet, popularised in the early seventies by one of the posh Sundays.

I remember little about it now in detail except that every meal had to be prefaced by half an unsweetened grapefruit.

The idea, I think, was that whatever food one ate, be it steak or salad or green vegetables, or the fried egg and bacon one was obliged to plough through for breakfast, it reacted in some violent way to the acid of the grapefruit. This, in turn, acted on the adipose tissue in question, which in some mysterious way dissolved. Or didn't, depending on your luck.

This diet, though certainly effective in my case (I lost ten pounds in as many days), had one or two in-built drawbacks. The first was a need for a permanent supply of grapefruit. Whether or not I really would have blown up like a Michelin man the instant I wavered one vitamin from the prescribed dietary scenario, as I feared, I cannot say. At all events, I was not about to suffer for over a week and then chuck it all away in a moment of weakness, and I remember going to astonishing lengths to ensure my thrice-daily intake of juicy Jaffa.

Namely the occasion on which I took a supply of grapefruit with me in my wash-bag when I went to stay with some friends in the country, and kept disappearing mysteriously to my room just as a meal was on the table. So panic-stricken was I at the possibility of the family not going in for cooked breakfasts that I actually crept downstairs, cooked and ate the slimming e and b and was back in bed again in time for two more hours of much-needed sleep. Unfortunately, although I carefully aired the kitchen both during and after this clandestine repast, the smell of cooking still lingered when my hostess descended at eight to prepare the coffee and croissants.

Being a gentleman, of course I owned up. She did not, however, take it as well as I had hoped.

'If we are not giving you the quantity of food to which you are clearly accustomed,' she said, 'then you have only to say so.'

I didn't see a lot of them after that.

In the years that followed I thought often about repeating my dietary triumph, but somehow the motivation wasn't there. I longed to melt away that spare tyre before it was too late, but simply couldn't bring myself to go through all the agony of turning down good dinner invitations and dreaming of pork pies – a dish that under normal circumstances rarely passes my lips, curiously enough.

And then, a couple of years ago, I was researching a book on sex in Britain today (*The Crisp Report*/Arrow/£1.25 – 'Matthew's best yet' – *Punch*) when I happened to ask the distinguished hair-dresser, Mr Ricci Burns, no stranger to the world of beautiful people, what one had to do to make oneself attractive to the opposite sex – or indeed to one's own kind, depending on one's inclination.

His answer was short and to the point, and it is one that many a middle-aged man could do a great deal worse than note down, ponder and act upon.

'Buy yourself a beautiful pair of jeans,' he said, 'and a smashing T-shirt. Treat yourself to a really great haircut. And go on a diet.' This is hardly the sort of advice to which a man of my years and position is guaranteed to respond with unquestioning enthusiasm. However, in the interests of research, I went ahead as per instructions.

Compared with most diets, this one proved simple to follow, never unpalatable, and astonishingly effective.

It consisted of an orange and a cup of black coffee for breakfast, an apple and cottage cheese for lunch, and meat or fish and green vegetables or salad for dinner. Every other day, you have meat or fish and vegetables or salad for lunch as well as for supper.

It had the added advantage that my wife was not obliged to stock up with an inordinate number of exotic items like two dozen avocado pears every three days, or thousands of lemons which had to be squirted over everything in sight. Indeed, serious dieters may argue, with some degree of justification, that it is scarcely a *diet* at all – a point of view that had certainly not escaped my greedy eye.

On the other hand, it had all the in-built disadvantages that accompany any drastic attempt to cut down on all those little pleasures that make life bearable – coffee and biscuits at eleven, Kit Kats and Bounty Bars after lunch, a slice of Jamaican ginger cake at four thirty, a whisky and soda of an early evening, a bowl of corn flakes before retiring at night.

For nearly a fortnight my family was forced to live with a bad-tempered man who couldn't get on with his work for thinking of how hungry he was, who ruined every meal by staring mournfully throughout at everyone else's plates, and bored everyone and himself rigid with long-winded discussions about what was fattening and what wasn't.

He also suffered from an advanced case of halitosis, so peculiarly pungent that it cleared whole rooms in seconds and put paid to his love life for weeks.

However, it all ended happily for everyone concerned, because when his wife finally brought herself to return to his arms, it was to find to her pleasure and his self-esteem that they were attached to a body which, although not quite as whippet-thin as he had hoped, was a stone and a quarter lighter than it had been for years.

And yet, when all's said and done, one wonders whether dieting, except in the cases of the grossly overweight, is really worth the candle after a certain age.

I have never met a middle-aged man yet who, within a week or two of awarding himself a personal Nobel Prize for Self-Discipline, is not complaining bitterly that once again his waistband is playing havoc with his kidneys and that when he sits on the loo, he cannot see into the pan for stomach.

Middle-age spread is a genuine fact of life. Containable perhaps, but after about the age of forty, pretty well unavoidable. The flesh can resist the pull of gravity for so long, but the time comes at last when even the firmest marble bum must begin to spread across the chair leather, the Michelangelic pectorals must melt into Rubensesque folds, and gradually from the firm banana of youth emerges the over-ripe pear of middle age.

Health Farms and Hydros

Despite an instinctive feeling that institutions of this sort encourage far too many of the weaknesses in character which have contributed to the moral decline of Western civilisation over the last fifty years – viz: self-indulgence, laziness, the belief that success can be achieved more easily through the spending of money than through application, hard work and self-denial, to name but a few – and should probably be banned by law, I must admit that the idea of spending a week in a hydro has always appealed to me enormously.

To think that for something between £200 and £300 (a modest enough outlay these days when a meal for two at some restaurants can cost you anything up to £100) you can lose as much as a stone in weight, rid yourself of toxins and poisons that have been cluttering up the system for months, tune up flabby muscles, some of which you never knew you owned, catch up on the days of lost sleep you thought you'd never know again, and one way and another make yourself sexually attractive to women . . . well, the prospect is tempting.

Indeed, ten years ago, at the urging of a fellow journalist who was feeling thoroughly pleased with himself following a week's stay at a health farm called Forest Mere, somewhere in Hampshire, and at the invitation of the principal, I actually undertook to try the place out for a few days in return for a few favourable paragraphs in a leading Sunday newspaper.

I remember the most beautiful September weather; the agony of the hot water and lemon diet that I was asked to submit to for the first day and a half; the sheer pleasure with which I lingered over my first yoghurt, honey and wheat-germ; a round of golf I played on a local course with one of the most blinding headaches I have ever known; an American song-writer who, when I asked him why no one had ever thought of raiding the kitchen garden for fruit and vegetables, replied, 'It's mined'; the alarming occasion on which I courteously invited a middle-aged lady for a quiet evening row on the lake (row as in boat, you understand), only to realise too late that she had quite different ideas in mind; the discovery that massages, when properly administered, are nothing like as soothing and gentle as I had imagined . . .

My strongest and most abiding memory, however, was of the limbering-up session that I joined at six o'clock on my first morning. It was led by the principal himself and took place on the lawn beside the lake. The grass was sodden with dew and an early morning mist lay low across the whole garden, presaging another perfect day and obscuring the outlines of the half dozen patients taking part.

I was particularly struck by the figure of a short, rather plump girl with long dark hair whom I could vaguely make out myopically through the mist on the far said of the circle we had been asked to form. She reminded me of someone I knew. A girl from Norfolk called Virginia perhaps? But no, her face was too refined for Virginia's, her eyes too large . . . Oddly enough, she looked a bit like a young Ava Gardner.

It was only as we were all strolling up towards the house for our first glass of hot water and lemon and the group drew together that I realised it *was* Ava Gardner. Not only that, but I actually had her completely to myself for the entire four minutes it took us to cross the lawn. My mind raced wildly as I tried to think of all the questions any self-respecting hack would ask Ava Gardner, were he by some astonishing stroke of fortune to find himself walking with her across the lawns of a health farm in Hampshire at six thirty in the morning: is Frank Sinatra really a sweet gentle human being at heart? Is Micky Rooney really as small as that? Was it true she has given up making pictures? How *about* Humphrey Bogart in *The Barefoot Contessa*?

In the end it was Ava who broke the silence.

'What sort of treatments are you having?' she said.

'Sauna, massage and I'm still debating whether to go for Slendertone. How about you?'

I couldn't for the life of me tell you what her reply was. Nothing worth valuable column inches anyway. I also cannot remember whether it was on that or a subsequent occasion that we discussed our diets. Being who she was, she had taken an ultra-private room away from the main building, so we bumped into each other less frequently than we might have. Whenever we did meet, however, the conversation turned immediately to one or other of the many problems that obsess everyone who enters the enclosed Order of Hydromaniacs – that is to say, hunger, weight loss, headaches, the massage table, the light diet room, the hilarious agony of it all .

Up till then, I would never have believed it possible that one day I would be able to tell my children that I learnt one of the basic principles of life from Ava Gardner, but I did and it goes as follows: when normally capable people are thrown together into a world in which they have paid a great deal of money in order to acquire a peripheral expertise of which they have no knowledge – be it a ski resort, the Lew Hoad Tennis School in Spain, or a health farm – their minds and bodies are concentrated to a degree that they rarely, if ever, achieve at any other time during the year. So much so that conversation on any topic other than the one in hand is more or less out of the question.

It is this practical application of the old principle that a change is as good as a rest, carried to the nth degree, that accounts for the success of health farms and hydros. That, and the fact that, no matter how flabby and unfit and thoroughly gross you may appear to others in the outside world, once beyond the reception area and into the towels and dressing gowns in which patients spend nearly all their days, and on to a sun-bed beside the swimming pool and the jacuzzi, suddenly, for the first time for years, you realise that

(a) there are an awful lot of people beside whom you feel like Fred Astaire at his prime and (b) even if you are not in fact Fred Astaire but Fred Emney, no one is ever going to notice.

If I seem to have committed a complete *volte-face* after my remarks at the very start of this chapter, I make no apologies for it. The insider's view of a health hydro, as anyone who has ever spent any time in hospital will readily appreciate, is very different from the outsider's. In fact I would go so far as to say that anyone contemplating a week of expensive fasting and pummelling would be ill-advised to make a preliminary recce. I carried out one recently as a part of my tireless research on behalf of my readers, at a hydro called Inglewood near Newbury in Berkshire.

Perhaps it is vivid memories of the scene in the James Bond film in which Old Hairy-Chest was nearly done to a turn in one of those individual Turkish baths by evil hands unknown, or perhaps I once watched an episode of *The Avengers* in which an apparently innocent health hydro was used as a cover for some devilish machination or other, I don't know, but I have always found hydros, from the outside anyway, extraordinarily sinister places.

At all events, I felt hideously overdressed as I was shown through the long, twisting corridors of the stately house, past the beauty salon and the shop and into the swimming pool area with its Italianate interior roofs, its low arches leading to various treatment rooms and glittering pool around which patients in various states of undress and various degrees of ugliness lay on sun-beds in attitudes of resignation, awaiting a summons to some treatment room or other.

I could not, as I sat there waiting to meet the head of the place, have felt fitter if I'd tried. And then the principal appeared – Australian, whippet-thin, grinning knowingly at me with magnificent teeth beneath a heavy moustache that alone exuded more health than all his patients put together. He reminded me slightly of John Newcombe, the Australian tennis player, in comparison with whom every man is made to feel about as attractive as a wart.

If I felt demoralised just by shaking Mr Kirk's hand, I was feeling as lively as a slow loris by the time he had finished telling me what was wrong with me: shoulders too narrow, teeth don't meet all the way round, too much refined carbohydrate as a child, too many whisky and sodas as an adult etc. etc.

Was the fact that I was overweight and careless of my appearance generally really nothing more than a deliberate attempt to solve some deep-seated sexual problem – i.e. by getting out of it altogether? Did I know that someone had done a comparative study on urban and rural foxes and found that the urban ones who live mainly out of people's dustbins suffer from arthritis? Had it ever occurred to me that far more attention is paid to the feeding of racehorses than of people? Had I never realised that one must be healthy in order to enjoy the rotten things in life?

Sadly, the ten-minute sauna, the thirty-minute Swedish massage with Roberta, the guided tour of the house, the knowledge that among their satisfied customers they are proud to number Bruce Forsyth, Joan Collins, The Flying Lizards, June Whitfield and David Hamilton (*the* David Hamilton), the promise of a stone lost in seven days – all this, far from encouraging me to whip out my American Express card and book a week on the spot, merely confirmed me in my conviction that the sooner I got out of the place while the going was good, the better.

The thing that depressed me most about it all was the compliance with which the patients, without whom the place would presumably not exist, knuckle down to a discipline which not even the most ineffectual holidaymaker would put up with in a bad package hotel on the Costa Brava.

As we sat in a neighbouring pub, drinking beer and eating rather good home-made steak and kidney pie, and Mr Kirk reeled off, with undisguised glee, the standard diet for the week (see below), I could not resist a question that many an unfortunate patient must have asked himself in the agony of his night starvation pains: Why do people put up with it? Why does nobody rebel?

Back came the chilling response: Take their clothes away, give them nothing to eat and you've got them cold.

So stunned was I that he managed to wade in with a supplementary before I had had a chance even to formulate the next question.

I might have guessed it; it's all to do with guilt. These high-livers have only themselves to blame for the mess they're in; nothing must be allowed to obstruct the path of justice. Anyone who attempts to step out of line (e.g. by slipping out to the pub for beer and sandwiches, trying to bribe matron with £50-notes, leading daring midnight raids on the organic greenhouse etc.) must expect to be treated exactly as if he were an army deserter, with summary punishment – in this case instant expulsion. Once one patient shows the slightest sign of weakness when the going gets tough, there's no knowing who might be tempted to crack up next. Cowardice and a general crumbling of moral fibre can spread through a place like that in an afternoon.

And yet, and yet . . . One can theorise about the British never feeling they've really achieved something unless they've suffered great personal hardship first, or talk about the strange sense of euphoria that prolonged lack of food often produces in people. Perhaps an explanation for the lack of rebellious spirit is quite simply that the staff organise the patients' daily treatments in such a way that they barely have time to think about anything more constructive than whether their next excitement is a volcanic mud bath or a go in the jacuzzi.

But then, as I say, the outsider's view of health hydros is invariably jaundiced. Sitting at home that evening with a whisky and soda in my hand and a hamburger and a large baked potato almost on the table, and thinking of those wretched prisoners at Inglewood washing down their aspirins with yet another hot water and lemon, I could not have felt happier. Except that of course at the back of my mind there was the niggling thought that in a few day's time they'd all be a stone lighter and feeling like giants refreshed, and I'd be as plump and jaded as ever . . .

Health Foods

If you should sense a hint of rattiness creeping into my voice in the section that's about to follow, it's because I am one of those people whose reaction to being told they are doing something they shouldn't be doing and vice-versa is one of immediate irritation, not to say uncontrollable rage. Other, milder characters may bow to superior judgement, admit that they are nothing but snivelling, ignorant twerps and immediately take whatever remedy may be suggested, be it going on a diet or giving up tight underpants.

Nothing, however, is guaranteed to make a more forcible entrance up my nostrils than the merest hint in the conversation of health foods.

All right, so I *know* I should be eating vegetables untouched by human chemicals and whole-wheat bread and chickens reared on natural dung and I *know* I am slowly poisoning myself with white sugar and pork pies and frozen peas and Instant Whip and all the things that make life bearable. Don't think for a moment I don't. What I can't bear are those middle-aged, do-gooding cranks who imply that, thanks to their natural, health-giving, and largely uneatable diet, they are automatically fitter than I am and one way and another superior. Why, if they have felt so near death's door all their adult lives, have they not done something about it years ago? Why the late conversion? The damage has been done; they are as full of artificial colouring and monosodium glutamate as I am and no amount of farm-killed cabbage is going to persuade me that they are going to live a minute longer than I am.

Friends who have heard me waxing hot on this subject before may prefer at this stage to move on to the next chapter and find out how to survive gardening or parents-in-law; others of my age, who are not familiar with my work in the field of health-food bores and who are showing dangerous signs of being wooed over to a life filled with oat cakes and muesli and deep anxiety, would be well advised to read on.

My horror of health-food bores was born the day I accepted an invitation to spend the day with a couple who had given up an extremely jolly life in Fulham to return to nature in a converted cowman's cottage somewhere in the West Country.

I was not reassured to discover upon arrival that these two, whom I had remembered as being attractive and amusing in their little house off Fulham Broadway, had in a few months acquired the pinched, prematurely aged look of underprivileged agricultural workers from a Thomas Hardy novel. Worse, they appeared to have lost every vestige of humour.

Within seconds of my disembarking from my car, which had suddenly assumed hitherto unsuspected capitalist overtones, they were bombarding me with detailed information about organically grown fruit and vegetables to the doubtful accompaniment of home-brewed beer. Or at least that's what they said it was.

Lunch, which took an age to produce, turned out to be nothing more complicated than a thin lentil soup in rustic pottery bowls whose rough-hewn bases had evidently been designed to fit the contours of a heavily ploughed field rather than a pine table top, for all its knots and nodules. This was accompanied by hunks of wholemeal bread topped with what appeared to be road chippings, one particularly unyielding piece of which removed an entire filling, thus mercifully putting me out of the running for the vegetable pancakes and a fearsome-looking apple crumble.

From that day on, health foods has always been firmly associated in my mind with the whirl of the dirndl skirt, and the rough embrace of hand-thrown pots. And toothache. I've said it all before and I'll say it again: show me a health-food addict and I will show you a lank head of hair, an unmade-up face and a pair of calloused feet in open sandals. The husband's the one in the beard and jogging shoes, clutching the paperback on yoga. Health food, as my self-sufficient friends pointed out more than once, is very much a way of life. Not, I am happy to say, of mine.

It's not that I do not believe people when they tell me that, thanks to brown rice and wholemeal bread, they have waved goodbye for ever to constipation; or that mixed sea vegetables contain up to 25 per cent protein and fourteen times as much calcium as milk; or that the Chinese discovered the secret of soya beans 2,500 years ago. It's just that, like diets, health foods always seem to dominate the conversation to the exclusion of every other subject.

Entire magazines and libraries of books are devoted to the beneficial effects of wholefoods on the digestive tract, how to supplement your diet and ginger up underactive thyroids with bladderwrack, and a thousand ways with toadstools.

In a funny little nook (or is it a cranny, or possibly even a crannery?) just off London's Shaftesbury Avenue, called Neal's Yard, the health freaks gather to buy their bread made from stone-ground flours, using only organic English wheat and other whole grains, their goat's curd and strained Greek yoghurt, their organically grown fruit and vegetables, their seaweed shampoo and their herbal toothpaste, and to chat with other converts about the wonders of acupuncture and the Alexander Technique, aroma-therapy and homoeopathic medicine, bhagwan, exegesis and Bernard Levin.

I am delighted that people should seek enlightenment and even immortality in the world of meaningless mantras and vegetarian cheddar, just so long as they wouldn't be so smug about it and try to make me feel I'm missing something.

We're none of us going to live for ever, however much wholemeal bread we eat. If the Reaper decides to take me off at the knees at the age of fifty-six, then so be it. I really cannot believe that the occasional fish finger or bowl of Instant Whip is going to make a lot of difference one way or the other.

But then some of us like to live a little dangerously.

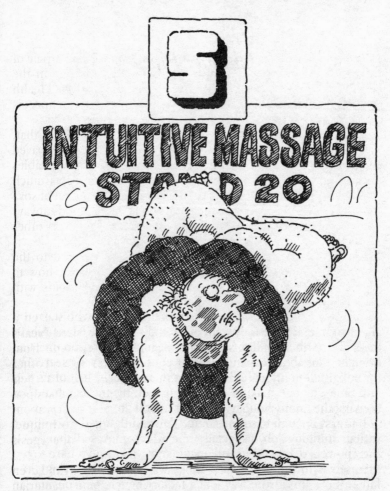

In which I expand my consciousness at the
Festival of Mind, Body and Spirit, consider
joining a Group Encounter Session, and
reveal my worst and most irrational
middle-aged worries.

Chapter Five

It was the Beatles who started it all, of course. Before they went off to India with the Maharishi to meditate on their millions and the meaning of life, no one had thought a lot about expanding their consciousness, or searching for enlightenment, or rediscovering themselves. Most of us had our time cut out making a living, or getting the car fixed, or booking the family holiday. Some of us still do.

It is easy enough to sound smug. The middle-aged who enjoy a varied, fulfilling job, especially one which makes demands on their powers of invention and imagination, may find it hard to put themselves in the position of those who earn their livings in a father more humdrum way – at a factory bench, pen-pushing in some office in the City, or selling life insurance. If those who are lucky enough to be paid for expressing themselves, as writers, actors or television producers have cause to stop from time to time and ask themselves what it's all about, how doubly keen must a middle-aged bank clerk be to find some answers.

It was more in a spirit, therefore, of disinterested research than of personal curiosity that in June of last year I hurried off to Olympia in West London for the Mind, Body and Spirit Festival of 1982 – 'The Show about you and me', as I was reminded by a sign in the foyer.

In fact, I could not have arrived in a more unreceptive state of mind, harrassed as I had been by a particularly bad series of traffic jams and a complete lack of parking meters, and irritated as I was by hanging about for over half an hour outside, having finally sneaked the car into an unobtrusive corner of a neighbouring back street, in the mistaken belief that I was to be joined by an equally middle-aged designer friend. It is at moments like this that one begins to wonder seriously about looking into the whole business of relaxation, mind control and possibly telepathy.

One also finds oneself asking oneself why it is that almost every person who pays his or her £2.50 entrance fee (half price after 6 p.m.) is so ferociously unattractive. A superabundance of open-toed sandals is always an ominous sign in my book; ditto a heavy turn-out of baggy jeans, T-shirts, flowery cotton numbers that look as if they were designed by Omar the Tentmaker, and straggly hair with beards and beads to match. One expects that of the young who eschew worldly values in favour of the spiritual, but I still find it hard to reconcile myself to the middle-aged and elderly dressed as if in constant search of the Woodstock pop festival.

Why is it that executives in Turnbull and Asser shirts and Gieves and Hawkes suits and Harrods haircuts do not appear to be on the lookout for enlightenment and inner consciousness? Or, for that matter, ladies in Jaeger skirts and rather good hats? Is it simply that those sort of people are too busy devising ways of paying for those sort of clothes? Or is it that the more unattractive you make yourself look, the more you feel the need to concentrate on your inner self?

It was in thoughtful mood that I made my way into the hall itself, in time to learn that I had just missed the Message to Mankind by People from Another Planet by the British Raelian Society.

However, there was plenty more on the menu that afternoon to interest the middle-aged man who felt sure there must be something in life more spiritually rewarding than the *Daily Telegraph* crossword on weekdays and Melvyn Bragg on Sundays.

I had hoped to have a quiet word with this fellow Benjamin Creme who claims that since 19 July 1977 Christ has been living in Britain – Brixton to be precise. Unfortunately, he was away from his stand at that precise moment. Still, I was given a very interesting demonstration of a machine that brings the freshness of mountain air into one's room twenty-four hours a day, and helps to relieve headaches, eczema, hay fever, sinus infections and tension. This was of particular interest to me after the trouble I had had with the traffic and I was delighted to note that, after taking only half a dozen breaths, I really began to feel quite relaxed.

So perky did I feel indeed that I was more than ready for the Raja Yoga meditation session at Stand B 23. I have often thought it could be very useful to be able to leave this earthly frame from time to time and fly to higher levels of awareness and I removed my shoes and settled down in the traditional cross-legged position along with a dozen other searchers after truth.

After a minute of two, an old, slightly bearded Indian woman sat down opposite us and cast her eye over us in an inscrutable sort of way. A young woman in a white sheet then spoke to us through a loudspeaker. She explained that the object of the exercise was to go beyond our bodies and through an old lady into union with the Supreme Being. I'm paraphrasing, of course, but you get the drift. I think she said the old lady's name was Daddy, but it was difficult to hear clearly above the noise in the hall.

The girl then put down her microphone. After a while, a totally disembodied voice told us that by concentrating carefully on what was said, we should find it easier to catch Daddy's vibrations and thus discover our true selves and the nature of our internal relationship with the Supreme Being. I wondered for a moment if this was perhaps the S. B. Himself speaking to us, but then realised it was coming from a tape recorder.

I can't remember everything that was said now. Roughly précised, it boiled down to a matter of stepping away from one's costume and seeing one's body separated from oneself so that one was able to fly into a world of gold and red light where there was nothing but silence and peace. That sort of thing.

Unfortunately, much as one tried to enter the spirit of the proceedings, the silence and peace one should soon have begun to experience was rudely shattered by the demonstration of Dancercise ('choreographed keep-fit and dance for people of all ages') that had just started up next door.

As a result I was in no mood to join the long queue of meditatees who were invited to approach Daddy and accept a special sweet that had been prepared in a state of meditation, and thus take even more soul and God-consciousness from her. I have always been brought up never to take sweets from a stranger, even one called Daddy, and besides, if I didn't stand up soon and move about, my legs would become completely paralysed, possibly for ever.

As it was, I was so stiff that I was seriously tempted to invest

£8.50 in an Intuitive Massage at the capable hands of Wally Gadalla on Stand G 20. However, time was running short and I was keen to have a Biorhythm Reading before I left.

All you had to do was to tell the lady on Stand A30 the date of your birthday, hand over a quid and a computer would immediately produce a chart outlining your physical, intellectual and emotional high and low spots for the coming months.

This was as exciting an offer as I have come across in years and I am only sorry that, although the lady carefully diagnosed my reading for me, and even went so far as to do me a free chart showing how compatible I am with my wife, I cannot now make head or tail of it.

It would appear that I had an emotionally critical day on 4 July and intellectually I was a bit dodgy on the 14th (something to do with the French, I daresay), but beyond that and the fact that physically I am well below par compatibility-wise, I can throw no further light on what I seem to remember was a most fascinating demonstration of 'an exciting new personal science'. It is a pity they can't outline one's memory cycle at the same time.

On my way out, I tried a small sample of some stuff called Spirulina which is 'a special form of vegetable plankton, which drifts in the currents of highly alkaline lakes or man-made growing ponds in various semi-arid regions around the world' and is said to be the most nutritious organic food known to man.

I certainly did not go away feeling like Popeye after a bowl of spinach. On the other hand, there was a definite perkiness in my step that had been sadly lacking for a good half hour.

I would have headed for home there and then had my eye not been caught by a stand selling self-hypnosis tapes and offering a free demonstration to show that, 'If you want to stop smoking, lose weight, be more successful in your job or even become better at your favourite sport or pastime, self-hypnosis tapes can help you'.

Only a fool could turn a blind eye to a promise like that. Not that any of the specific problems mentioned were directly relevant to me personally. At the same time I have noticed in myself an increasing fondness in recent months for police series on television, and I was interested to know whether this might be one way of stamping on it before it got completely out of control and I found myself signing on as a Special Constable.

After a short wait, I was shown to a chair and had a pair of headphones clamped over my ears. The people on either side of me were apparently in an advanced state of self-hypnosis. A deep, rather oily voice then murmured: 'Close your eyes, follow the instructions and you will have a super ten minutes.'

I certainly did. I couldn't tell you how others of my age, education, background etc. would react in similar circumstances. All I know is that I went out like a light and awoke to hear the voice saying, 'Congratulations, and welcome to a beautiful day'.

I have no idea what subconscious messages were oozed into my dormant brain, but I have never felt happier and fresher in my life and could not resist mentioning the fact to the elderly woman in the next chair who had finished just ahead of me. 'Good for you,' she said. 'My feet are still killing me.' The man on the other side said he felt fine adding, 'But then I'll fall for anything. That's my whole trouble.' I couldn't help noticing that he was wearing a very badly fitting wig.

As I made my way across Kensington High Street towards my car, I was rather nervous that the hypnotist with the oily voice might have tried to make a monkey out of me while I was out and that suddenly, for no reason whatsoever, I would think I was a chicken and try to lay an egg on a zebra crossing. Or assault a traffic warden.

As it happened, I was sorry he hadn't, since I arrived at my car to find I had a parking ticket. I was in such a fury that, while reaching across to rear off the offending piece of paper from my windscreen, I ricked my neck badly and gave myself such a bad headache in the rush-hour traffic going home that I arrived there feeling even worse than I had before the exhibition.

Still, I discovered more about inner consciousness during the miserable twenty minutes I spent stuck in a jam in the North End Road than I'd learnt in three hours among the experts and yogis and prophets and healers in Olympia. But then when it comes down to it, isn't that what it's really all about?

Group Encounter Sessions

I realise that these sort of exercises are popular among certain more emotional and probably oversexed middle-aged men who feel they have a communication problem. Personally, I have never felt the slightest urge to spend an expensive weekend in some draughty country house being shouted at by my wife and worrying about my failure to come up to scratch as a husband, father, lover and human being. I can get all that at home for nothing.

Irrational Fears and Worries

I have always been a great worrier. As a small boy, I worried about having dirty hands and being bashed up by gangs of village boys. As a teenager, I worried about my spots. I spent much of my early manhood convinced that I had been unaccountably struck down with impotence.

Happily, that was one fear that was proved to be entirely without foundation, and in my mid-thirties I spent several wretched days in the sure belief that the unexpected change in my National Health spectacles prescription could only be explained by my having mysteriously contracted venereal disease. However, I soon put that out of my mind when the headaches started up and I spent more than one sleepless night trying to pluck up the courage to have a brain scan.

I cannot now recall the worry that eventually superseded that one. Possibly the insect bite that I knew for certain had turned septic and would carry me off in a matter of days, like Rupert Brooke my early promise still unfulfilled and my looks but a faint memory in the minds of many a sorrowing female. Possibly not.

All I know is that, until I approached middle age, I had barely begun to realise the full extent of my worry potential. If someone had told me ten years ago that it was possible for anyone in his right mind to consider becoming a vegetarian rather than run the risk of choking to death on a piece of lamb bone, I would have dismissed him as a hysterical crank. Now, of course, I recognise him for the wise and perceptive bird he obviously was.

Any family man of my age who never worries himself sick that at any moment he might trip over the dog while coming downstairs holding the baby, or that the VAT inspector is going to demand proof that the portable colour television set was essential to one's development as a short-story writer, or that the next door's cat is going to dig up the antirrhinum seedlings, should *really* start worrying.

Those, on the other hand, who can honestly admit that any empty spaces that might conceivably be left in their minds are fully given over to worrying, can consider themselves to be well and truly middle-aged, and I can do no better than direct them towards the most useful and comprehensive guide to worry so far devised: Robert Morley's *Book of Worries*.

The most cursory glance through the list of contents is enough to reassure the most anxious that here is a man who has their interests totally at heart – Arrest, Wrongful; Assault, Indecent; Botulism; Constipation; Knocks on the Door; Lavatory Seats; Tourniquets; Wills . . . The ground is well covered.

To these I should like to add a few of my own, to help to convince fellow worriers that they are not alone.

1. Being burgled by the minicab driver who arrives to collect you and your luggage and run you to Heathrow when you are off on your holiday. I have a long, carefully prepared speech which I launch into the moment we turn into Nightingale Lane (I don't actually live in Nightingale Lane, by the way, or really anywhere near it; I just mentioned that by way of example, as I might mention Kentish Town Road or Beaufort Street). This includes references to the burglar alarm system being wired up to the local police station, the black belt karate expert who lives in the house when we're not there, the puff adders, and the fact that I am an extremely badly paid male nurse. It seems to have paid off so far (the speech, that is, not being a male nurse), but then, of course, there's always the milkman to worry about. And is the message on the answering machine about 'being back shortly' really convincing . . . ?

2. Having recently watched the film *Brief Encounter* again on television, I have this premonition that, any day now, my wife could set off for an innocent morning's shopping in Peter Jones, get a bit of dust caught in her eye in Sloane Square at the very moment that a doctor from South Kensington happens to be passing on his way to W. H. Smith and . . . But how far-fetched can you get? The real worry, of course, is how many young doctors go off to Africa these days?

3. The reason I have given up bathing in the sea in East Anglia isn't really because I know that most Great White Shark attacks occur in less than three feet of water. Even so, it is an interesting fact, isn't it?

4. I was once told on very good authority that you should always unplug the television set at night, rather than just switch it off. I am not sure whether this is because the electricity can continue to leak imperceptibly into the back of the set while one is asleep, thus causing it to overheat and eventually burst into flames, or what. All I know is that once I went away without unplugging it and spent the entire weekend telephoning the house at hourly intervals on the principle that as long as the ringing tone was in order,

so was the house, but the instant I got unobtainable, I'd know the telephone had melted along with everything else.

5. I may not be a household name exactly, but anyone who writes or broadcasts these days, however infrequently, is liable to be a potential target for some fanatical political group, and, whatever my wife may say, I still refuse to accept that I was over-reacting by asking the police to pop around and open that sinister-looking package for me the other day. All right, so it turned out to be a second-hand book I had ordered six weeks previously, but it was not my fault that I didn't recognise the postmark. It is not as though I go to Yoxford every day of the week.

6. The older I get, the more I worry about losing all control in a traffic jam and being seized by an uncontrollable impulse to ram every other vehicle in sight. Ditto pedestrians.

7. Having recently acquired an unerring talent for stepping into dog do-es every time I go out of the house, I worry that one of these days I'm going to walk one into every room of the house before noticing.

8. Cancer. Robert Morley is right, as usual, when he says, 'Cancer worry is like the late Henry Irving: in a class by itself. It takes precedence over approaching blindness or loss of hearing, personal failure of any kind, the weather and the life hereafter. There is something seriously wrong with you if you do not imagine you have cancer at least once a month.' Strictly speaking therefore this is not a worry to which I can possibly lay sole claim. On the other hand, is it my imagination or did I hear somewhere that one of the symptoms can be *gaining* weight?

9. I am not sure which is worse: suffering in silence as a local gang of ten-year-olds pull bits off my privet hedge, or letting them feel the sharp side of my tongue and then living in an agony of suspense, waiting for the first scratch to appear down the side of my Citroen Safari.

10. I am convinced that it is only a matter of time before I give in to an irrational and overwhelming urge to shout out some expletive during a quiet moment in a concert in the Royal Festival Hall.

In which I point out the perils of being a
Last Chance Trendy and describe what the
forty-five-year-old man-about-town should
and should not be wearing if he wishes to
retain his youthful good looks without
making himself appear to be a refugee from
the sixties.

Chapter Six

We have now reached the point in this modest little account of middle-aged life when I must introduce you to that familiar and pathetic figure of our time, the LCT. The Last-Chance Trendy.

He's the one who, in a highly excitable state of pre-menopausal panic, grabs at every scrap of passing stylistic driftwood (not to say a certain amount of debris that should have sunk without trace years ago) in the hope of persuading the rest of the world, and himself, that he is as much in the swim of things as ever he was. Or, if he never was, then he would like to be before it is all too late.

You can't miss the LCT. He's the one who sends his jeans to the dry cleaners and wears his figure-hugging shirts unbuttoned to the breastbone, the better to display the gold bullion nestling among the greying chest hairs. Often he wears running shoes and brightly coloured socks; sometimes a denim jacket and an Indian silk scarf gathered at the throat in a small gold ring.

His hand-tooled leather belt does not, as he believes, mark him out as the possessor of the secret of eternal youth. On the contrary, it merely draws attention to the paunch that oozes over the waistband like baker's dough from a bread tin. As for those two pieces of fat just above the kidneys which the French, with typical continental extravagance, refer to as *les poignées d'amour* (the handles of love), these have reached a point where only a lady with hands the size of a pound of pork sausages could seriously be attracted.

The hair, or such of it as remains after it has been trained down the cheekbones in slabs of grey, or up and over the cranium in an unconvincing attempt to disguise the bald patch, hangs lank and unmodish over the ears and sometimes the collar.

The equally outdated Zapata moustache adds yet another splash of grey to the already rocky complexion, and the nervous Gitane merely adds to the halitosis and increases the chances of a heart attack before the age of fifty.

We shall be hearing more about the LCT and his ill-advised attempts to keep pace with the younger generation later in the book, but for the moment I shall be confining my comments to his unfortunate notions concerning dress and appearance. And if, as a result of what I have to say, just a few of my contemporaries are dissuaded from making themselves look even more foolish than they need be, then I shall feel that my work will not have been in vain.

Happily, I have found a fellow anti-LCT activist in the slim and maddeningly youthful shape of the men's fashion expert and author of *The Vogue Fitness Book for Men* Mr Geoffrey Aquilina-Ross. Rather than burden you with a verbatim account of our conversation together, let me summarise the main points of our findings:

1. The Body

Do not be fooled into supposing that because one's weight has not altered in fifteen years, neither has one's shape. Chests, whether you like it or not, drop; backs fatten; bums spread. From a purely physical point of view, therefore, the middle aged can never hope to compete with youth and any attempts to do so with fitted shirts (or darted, as they were known in their heyday), hipster trousers, etc. are bound to end in sartorial disaster. Most middle-aged men are at least five to six pounds overweight and all too frequently appear to be making every effort to remind one of the fact.

2. The Bum

Some years ago the *Sunday Times* carried out a survey in which they pinpointed the parts of the male anatomy that women found sexually exciting – in order of ogleability, as it were. Top of the pops by a mile was the small, tight bum, a choice that would appear to have changed little over the years to judge by the fondness of today's young for baggy shirts underpinned by tiny buttocks and snake-like hips.

Bums are still very much in, in every sense of the word – except, of course, after a certain age whereupon they are very much out. This accounts for the struggle so many of us have fitting all our extraneous flesh into clothes from shops like Take Six, The Village Gate, Lord John and other well-known suppliers to the anorexic. Several years ago I had my head turned by a nineteen-year-old who, in an effort to divest me of the baggy cords in which I happily passed most of my leisure hours, inveigled me into one of these shops and into a pair of trousers that appeared to have been designed for a twelve-year-old. Shocked and pained by the extent to which certain more obvious parts of my anatomy made their presence felt, I could not resist making some pointed comment to this effect to the sales assistant. 'The cluster,' he replied, 'is prominent these days.' I shall have more to say about the dangers inherent in middle-aged men taking up with very much younger women in a later chapter. Suffice to say at this stage that I, unlike many I could name but won't, never again attempted to steel myself to the dwarfish crutch, and I cannot pretend to be anything other than thoroughly happy with my decision.

3. Bell-bottomed trousers

These are strictly out for anyone faintly interested in cutting anything of a sartorial dash. Ditto hipsters. Anyone caught wearing a pair of either can almost certainly be said to be middle-aged, since only the middle-aged, with their parsimony born of ration books and long contact with an older generation for whom looking after one's clothes and making them last was a way of life, would even think of hanging onto garments that they bought in the sixties.

4. Jeans

Whatever Ricci Burns may say, men over forty should wear these only at home when carrying out private menial tasks like gardening, doing the VAT or hanging wallpaper. Exceptions to the rule include rehearsing actors, out-of-work actors earning the rent as dailies, American cowpokes, and film people, few of whom appear to have got much further in their dress sense than flower power. Where else these days can you find a more concentrated collection of beards, necklaces, chains, denim, heavily tinted granny glasses, Zapata moustaches and girls in peasant Indian dresses and cowboy boots smoking Gitanes than in a film production meeting?

5. Denim jackets

No man over forty should be seen dead in a denim jacket. Men of sixty to seventy who wear them probably *are* dead.

6. Shoes

The middle-aged man who sacrifices comfort on the altar of fashion is a fool to himself and his chiropodist. The older one gets, the more fragile one's feet, and if one cannot afford to have one's shoes made by Tricker or Lobb's, the least one owes one's old friends is a decent pair of bench-turned Church's – preferably lace-up for extra comfort. Personally I have long been a vociferous champion of the chukka boot and stupidly allowed myself to be talked out of them for over ten years by the same teenager (see above) who tried to prove against all the odds that three into two *will* go. I tried to tell her that my desert boots, hand-crafted by Duckers of The Turl in Oxford, were not Hush Puppies, but she was not to be persuaded. 'You can tell everything about a man from his shoes, ' she declared. 'And men who wear flabby Hush Puppies usually have flabby whatsits.' Why I should have been taken in by this specious sociological footnote I cannot imagine, but I was – even though I threw the girl out soon after the chukkas. I completely lost touch with her after that, and for ten long years my feet were a stranger to suede. And then, a month or two ago, my eye was drawn to an advertisement in one of the Sunday colour supplements by a firm in Surrey selling cut-price, good quality chukkas for only £7.99. On a whim I sent off for a pair. I thought they might come in useful for walking long distances along the beaches of East Anglia. Not wishing to wear them out in advance, I kept them for some time in a box in my wardrobe. One day I had to pop up to the Marylebone Road to do something and decided, for no particular reason, to take the opportunity to try them out. Who should I bump into near Baker Street station but the same teenager, now aged twenty-nine and none the less attractive for that. Her eyes at once homed in on my feet . . . I tried to explain to her about it being the first time I'd worn a pair of chukkas in ten years and about being married and having the children and so on, but I just know she didn't believe me . . .

7. Shirts

Again, avoid sixties boutiques. The quality is not that good and they nearly always skimp on material, which means that the sleeves are so tight on a man of my age that at best he is unable to raise his arms above his shoulders and at worst he runs a serious risk of gangrene of the fingers. Also, every time he moves his body in any direction from the vertical, he exposes a broad strip of flabby waistline.

8. Underpants

Nine out of ten middle-aged men look deeply unattractive in traditional Y-front pants and grotesque in mini-briefs. Tight underwear is also, as everyone knows only too well who has ever worn it, a major cause in this country of sterility among males aged twenty-five to forty-five, not to say prickly heat and dhobi itch. All of which may well account for the fact that most men's underpants are bought by women. (For men, you understand.) Hence, presumably, the fact that my wife presented me about a year ago with three pairs of Marks & Spencer 'jockey shorts'. Quite why she should have been so convinced that these would provide a satisfactory substitute for my highly serviceable briefs I am not quite certain. I have a feeling she must have seen some American film star wearing them in a situation that for some reason caught her imagination. Or conceivably a jockey.

While I am prepared to believe that this style of underwear can transform certain men from flabby accountants into Paul Newman (or even Willie Carson) look-alikes, there are others of us who, for inexplicable physiological reasons, slip on the 'jockeys' with immense confidence only to find we more closely resemble Walter Matthau at his most hangdog.

Perhaps it was the way they were washed, I really couldn't say, but after a month or two the leg length began to increase to such an extent that I soon became the only man I knew who went around in broad daylight secretly wearing a ra-ra skirt under his trousers.

Eventually the shame became too much for both of us to bear and my wife rushed off to Harrods and came back with several pairs of 'Sunspels' – lighter-weight affairs altogether and strangely Newmanesque – although I doubt that even he would be prepared to splash out £4.25 of his hard-earned salary on an item of clothing as functional as a pair of 'undershorts', as I believe they refer to them in the United States.

And yet, who knows? I understand there is a shop in South Molton Street, W1, where it is possible to buy a pair of underpants for £14. The explanation would seem to be that they have been designed by someone called Giorgio Armani. Though how something as simple as a pair of underpants could possibly be 'designed' – even by someone with as expensive a sounding name as that – I fail to comprehend. Nor do I have the financial resources or the energy to find out. Is it any wonder that the population figures in this country are dropping at the rate they are?

9. Suits

Like many a middle-aged Englishman who lived through the war years and for whom the word 'saving' conjures up images of powdered eggs and utility marks on woollen underwear rather than Ray Clemence in action, I suffer from a deep-seated and irresistible need to hang on to clothes far longer than is desirable, either aesthetically or hygienically. I also have a completely distorted idea of how much one should be paying for them.

My personal costings are based on prices in about 1962. Thus, until recently, I fondly believed that a pair of cavalry twill trousers should cost about £5, a shirt £3, a pair of walking shoes £4, and a suit £40, top whack.

In fact, it was still possible to buy a perfectly decent suit from

Take Six or The Village Gate for under £35 in the early seventies – to wit the black double-breasted number into which I was slipping happily and comfortably for all manner of formal occasions, including my own wedding, until only a few months ago. All right, so perhaps the trousers are a little on the wide side by today's standards. Ditto the lapels. But all in all I reckon it was £32.50 very well spent indeed.

It was with enormous reluctance therefore that I finally allowed myself to be talked by my wife into a visit to Messrs Gieves and Hawkes, the distinguished firm of naval and military tailors in Savile Row. Their Mr Ward opened the proceedings by announcing that no man of my age and position can be considered well attired unless he has at least six suits in his wardrobe – three dark formal suits, one general all-purpose flannel suit and two tweed suits for the weekend.

I laughed and pointed out that no one can wear more than one suit at a time.

Mr. Ward said that, more to the point, no one can wear one suit all the time without very soon looking extremely shabby. 'No matter how much you pay for a suit,' he said, 'you must give it a chance.'

I couldn't resist commenting that my own suit still looked exactly the same as the day I bought it. Mr Ward agreed that that was unfortunate. 'Not bad cloth,' he said, feeling the lapel between his fingers. 'You ought to have it made up into a suit,' and went on to tell me a pointed story about a customer who came in to complain that a blazer he had had made there twenty-six years previously was showing signs of wear. When Mr Ward politely suggested that the chap might consider a new one, he replied, 'I'm afraid I cannot justify the outlay for a new garment at present.' I didn't like to say so, but he had my total sympathy.

Anyway, I allowed myself to be talked into considering two suits – a charcoal grey double-breasted flannel for business, dinner parties etc., and a fine Glen Urquhart three-piece for travelling and weekends. While I was about it, I also picked out a tweed jacket, a camel overcoat and a pair of cavalry twills. One never knows when one might not be invited to a point-to-point.

Mr Ward was very keen that I should have one of the suits run up in a very fine worsted known as Super 100s. He told me that it's the sort of quality that has women crossing the room just so that they can touch you. Personally, I have never encouraged strange women to touch me, nor would I welcome it were it ever to occur and I told him that the usual material was good enough for me.

A Mr Jordan then came and took my measurements.

I said, 'The thirty-six-inch waist may be rather misleading. The fact is, I'm carrying a little excess weight at present.'

Mr Ward said that almost everyone of my age who came into the shop said that, and that what he usually suggested was that they should make the trousers slightly on the large side and then take them in as and when the customer recovered his figure. I had no alternative but to fall in with his suggestion. A man of my age can deceive himself so far over his figure, but no further. Sooner or later he must face up to the truth, and clearly the sort of customers Gieves and Hawkes deal with are expected to be able to take it on the chin – or any other part of the body it happens to be delivered, which in my case appeared to be pretty well all over.

Fortunately, I am no stranger to harsh personal criticism, but even so, I felt that some of Mr Jordan's comments on my figure were slightly uncalled for. 'Hollow back' I can just about accept as a physiological fact of life, but 'Shoulders slightly sloping, off left'. . . I can only suppose I was standing awkwardly at the time. At all events, Mr Ward's jovial remark to the effect that I had got off lightly did little to raise my flagging spirits, any more than did the news that my modest ensemble came to just under £1,800.

I told him I'd like to think about it and set off for Soho where I made a few enquiries with a jobbing tailor I know re the possibility of having a pair of black suit trousers narrowed. Ditto lapels.

But, of course, once one has tasted good-quality tailoring, if only for a minute or two, it's not easy to accept second best. Luckily, I can still struggle into most ready-to-wear, size forty regulars, and the dark grey double-breasted I picked up in Gieves's winter sale has certainly imbued me with a sense of confidence that I never enjoyed in black wool from Take Six.

No women have yet crossed the room to feel my material, but it's early days yet.

10. Casual clothes

Stepping out on to the pavement after an excellent lunch at a well-known Chelsea wine bar with one of my more worldly middle-aged friends recently, my eye was caught by the sight of an astonishingly good-looking woman in her mid-thirties climbing into a Porsche which had been parked carelessly on a yellow line.

Hers, I am sorry to say, was not caught by the sight of me getting my leg over my Honda C50.

'What does a man of our age and talent and experience have to do,' I enquired of my friend, 'in order to make any sort of impact on a woman like that?'

'Simple,' he declared. 'Take yourself off to Fortnum & Mason with £500 in your pocket, treat yourself to a couple of sports jackets and a pair of decent trousers and any woman in London could be yours for the asking. Women like that can always tell a serious contender at a glance.'

I said, 'But this blazer of mine has come in for some extremely favourable comment in its time and I cannot think of any man I know who would not be happy to be seen in these grey flannel trousers.'

'I think,' said my friend, 'that it's probably the plastic motor-cycling outfit that lets you down.'

He may have had a point or he may not concerning the ensemble, but his advice relating to the drawing power of certain types of casual clothing certainly found an echo in the words of Geoffrey Aquilina-Ross.

'Any reasonably attractive middle-aged man always looks fabulous in casual clothes, provided he doesn't appear to be trying too hard,' he said. 'Slip into a plum-coloured Shetland and a well-cut pair of blue cords from somewhere like Jaeger or Austin Reed and you can't fail to make an impact.'

Maybe not if you happen to have nice broad shoulders and nice narrow hips and a nice small bum and youthful good looks and hair that never looks out of place and good teeth and no wives and children to cost you every penny you earn, so that all you can afford is what you can pick up at a C&A sale.

The fact is that anyone over the age of forty who finds himself in this happy position and for whom it is a matter of concern whether or not he makes an impression will probably do so dressed in a Shetland and blue cords or Albanian shepherd's clothes. It all boils down to this: do you look like a man of substance or a pratt? Beyond that I cannot really help you.

11. Hair and haircuts

The LCT still labours under the sad misapprehension that there is some correlation between long hair and long life. He is convinced that, like Samson, if he loses his locks he loses his looks – and hence his youth.

However, he knows that, if he goes the whole hog and turns up at client meetings looking like Billy Connolly, he could well find himself out on his invisible ear. So he compromises disastrously either with the earless, neckless look which makes him look like a relation of David Hamilton (*the* David Hamilton), or the Brillo Pad look which makes him look like a very old Kevin Keegan.

Speaking as one who has spent twenty years or more combing London and most counties south of a line drawn between the Bristol Channel and the Wash in search of the perfect haircut, I am only too well aware of the temptations. Instinct told me that by the age of about thirty-five I should be aiming for a style in keeping with my age and position in society, but fashion and slightly protruding ears lured me into a variety of establishments all of which appeared to understand the full significance of the words, 'Oh, just a light trim, please. Ha ha. Don't forget to leave it full round the back and sides will you?'

There was Aldo of Rome (or more precisely of Soho) who never used anything but a cut-throat razor, couldn't begin without washing the hair first and invariably sent one off looking like Tony Blackburn. There was Micky, the Greek Cypriot, in Battersea Park Road with a fag stuck permanently out of the corner of his mouth through which he would cough over his customers' heads. Since he had one eye permanently cocked in the direction of the racing on the television, it was a matter of astonishment to me that I never lost an ear, or worse.

Then there was the fancy dive somewhere near Grosvenor Square where a beautiful, busty girl from Golders Green transformed a simple hairwash into an experience slightly more sensual than a night out in Bangkok.

A young man at Annie Russell's chic unisex establishment in Chelsea had his moments too.

But all this was in my bachelor youth when I could afford such self-indulgence. More recently I had taken to patronising cheap and cheerful local shops with names like Harry's and Vic's, in whose windows the flies competed for space with the Gossamer Featherlites.

In fact it was *en route* to one such joint near me in Balham that I bumped into a woman friend of mine who said I ought to be ashamed of myself, a man of my age messing about in places like that. She swore by the Men's Hairdressing Department at

Harrods and suggested that I could do a great deal worse than make an appointment there myself.

How right she was. My Mr Leigh (I think I may refer to him in this rather proprietorial way now without giving undue offence; it was certainly the way I came to regard him after only a couple of visits) was and is the perfect hairdresser for the man of taste and distinction. After a lifetime of oily patronising ('And how does sir feel about the length on top?'), monosyllabic pressurisation ('Spray?'), snobbish small-talk ('Are we going north for the grouse this year, sir?'), polite terrorisation ('I have been cutting hair for thirty years, if you don't mind'), cosy neglect ('Relax, read a magazine, I'll get one of the girls to bring you a coffee'), and conspiratorial innuendo ('Will there be anything else, sir?'), it was with feelings of joy and disbelief that, possibly for the first time ever, I was able to sit in a barber's chair for ten minutes without once feeling compelled (a) to make conversation, (b) to mutter 'You're not taking *too* much off at the back there, are you?' and (c) to wonder if I'd need to raise a mortgage for the tip.

Mr Leigh never implies that if I don't have the shampoo first, then on my own head be it. He never pads round me, cocking his eye at my thatch like a bird reckoning his chances with a discarded ham sandwich and making lightning raids on odd areas behind my ears like tonsorial afterthoughts. He doesn't stand there for minutes on end, lovingly smoothing his handiwork into a fancy shape that one immediately destroys within moments of stepping into the street. And he never attempts to interfere with my personal family planning.

He knows exactly how my hair can be shown off to its best advantage, but he doesn't bully me into believing him. He simply gets on with it. And somehow he always achieves a feat that I had always dreamt about but finally told myself was unobtainable – that of cutting my hair in such a way that (a) it looks as though it was done a week ago, and (b) it doesn't need doing again for at least six weeks.

Eat your heart out, Aldo.

12. Handbags

'Ghastly' – Geoffrey Aquilina-Ross.

13. Jewellery

Anything gold that hangs round the neck and, more importantly, is *seen* to hang round the neck, marks you out at once as an LCT. If not, then a foreigner. Possibly both. Ditto earrings and identity bracelets. Traditional English gentlemen's jewellery on the other hand, worn discreetly and in the right places, is always reassuring: a slim watch on a good leather strap, a Dunhill cigarette lighter, a plain signet ring (see Wales, Prince of).

14. After-shave lotion

It seems scarcely believable now that in the mid-sixties I and many another young man about town seriously went to parties, dinner parties and even to the theatre in a cloud of Fabergé Brut as inpenetrable as a swarm of bees. Is it my imagination playing tricks or do I distinctly remember a well-known actress saying to me as we picked at our saltimbocca at the San Frediano, 'The faintest whiff of Brut has me swivelling my head looking for the wearer'? These days presumably she'd be looking for the exit.

Nowadays no self-respecting man over the age of forty dare be caught dead smelling of anything that is advertised on television or lingers on the shirt collar for more than a week. Unless, of course, he's an American. They like nothing better than a down-market smell at an up-market price.

I read somewhere the other day that an after-shave lotion called Denim is 'for men who don't have to try too hard'. In which case, why use anything at all?

I cannot pretend to be a great after-shave man these days. I have a vague memory of reading somewhere that women can tell everything about a man from his after-shave, but how is one to know which of the many hundreds of pongs on offer singles one out as a man of the world and which as a cheapskate? The advertisements are no help, however cleverly the stuff is dolled up. Take, for one, an eau de toilette called L'Homme by Roger & Gallet. It shows a husky-looking man without a shirt on, holding a hand to the back of his neck where he has presumably just slapped a bracing dose of the product in question.

According to the caption he is Denis S – 'A much travelled actor. He cares.' Though about what is not entirely clear.

The headline declares: 'L'Homme est rare', which is French

for 'The man is rare'. This French *jeu de mots* is presumably intended to imbue the product with a spurious air of sophistication.

The copy then goes on to inform us that, 'L'Homme Roger & Gallet Eau de Toilette has a quite different freshness. A solid freshness, derived from other sources. Not from the sharp notes of lemon, but the more exotic notes of spearmint, juniper berries, sage and coriander, rock-rose and ylang-ylang. A tumult of woody fragrances, with a hint of mischief from spices and labdanum. A strange, almost perplexing combination . . . out of the common run since 1806.'

All of which may do wonders for a well-travelled actor who cares, but could easily have one going around smelling like a lump of chewing gum in a health-food shop.

Speaking as one who has always believed in flying the flag, I suppose I should be recommending a no-nonsense native fragrance like Burberry's or Dunhill – something that comes in an old-fashioned, unpretentious bottle that, with all its inbuilt associations with tweed suits, dead pheasants and retrievers asleep in front of the fire, serves to remind one of what life in this great country of ours is really all about.

Unfortunately, I am not at present in a position to practise what I preach, having been given a large bottle of some stuff called Eau Sauvage which I simply can't seem to get through. Or, knowing how much it cost, to chuck down the sink.

In which I explore the perils and pleasures of being a middle-aged parent, be it of bright two-year-olds or bolshy teenagers, and offer words of wisdom on how and how not to keep up with the young – in the disco, on the turntable, astride the motorbike, and at the wheel of the sports car.

Chapter Seven

Twenty-five years ago, when I was a boy of eighteen fresh out of school, I took a turn, as one did in those days, as an assistant master at a boys' preparatory school in Sussex. I couldn't have enjoyed it more. On the one hand, I was a grown-up at last and, as such, could smoke a pipe and drink beer at the pub and drive up to town for a show on my day off and go to bed when I felt like it. At dinner with the head-master and his wife and the staff, the conversation was as sophis-ticated as the food. It was there that I first tasted avocado pear and acquired a penchant for *coquilles St Jacques*. There too I learned to play Real Tennis and ring a simple peal of church bells.

At the same time I was mentally little older than most of the boys and with them I was able to relive many childhood pleasures, like conkers, and learn one or two new skills such as hoola hooping.

Not surprisingly, discipline was often difficult to maintain. From the very first moment I walked into B2 and every boy in the form pretended to be the boy next to him, my relationship with my charges was poised constantly on a knife edge as I teetered wildly between total command and utter humiliation.

It was the seemingly innocent questions about sex that I most dreaded. 'Sir, please sir, what's circumcision sir?' 'You obviously know the answer perfectly well, Duvall, or you wouldn't be asking me in that silly voice.' 'Well, sir, I *sort* of know sir,' (Snigger smirk.) 'I just wanted to check that I'd got it right, sir.' 'And what do you think it means, Duvall?' 'Well, sir, according to Miss May, sir [the elderly Scripture teacher], it's the removal of the foreskin according to an ancient Jewish custom, sir.' 'What more can I tell you, Duvall?' 'Nothing, sir, except . . . Sir, do you suppose Miss May has had her foreskin removed according to an ancient Jewish custom?' 'I really wouldn't know, Duvall. You'd better ask her yourself.' Result: non-speaks with Miss May for three weeks.

The trouble was one never knew whether they were genuinely hungry for knowledge or simply trying to be funny.

'Sir, do you know why a cat puts its tail up when you stroke its back?' (Heart sinks.) 'No, Feltwell, I don't. Why does it?' 'Well, sir, if it didn't, your hand would fall off at the end, wouldn't it, sir?'

The point of this rather over-extended footnote to my early professional career is to demonstrate how early in life one is viewed as middle-aged by people one genuinely thinks of as one's contemporaries. Feltwell and I might happily have played conkers together in an idle moment on a Sunday afternoon, or discussed how best to skin a freshly caught mole, but I realise now that deep down he thought of me as just another stupid grown-up.

One day he enquired casually how old I was, sir.

'You tell me, Feltwell.'

'I don't know, sir.'

'Guess.'

'About forty-three, sir?'

If I was taken aback twenty-five years ago, it was as nothing compared with the dowsings in cold water to which I am constantly submitted now that I actually *am* forty-three.

The mistake I am always making is supposing the age gap between the generations is bound to narrow. All too frequently I have found myself among much younger people – at dinner perhaps or at a party – and even as I hold forth on some subject of general interest, such as the effect of the drop in world interest, rates or why David Gower cannot hold a candle to P.B.H. May, I am aware of all these youthful eyes upon me wearing expressions of pained disbelief as they metaphorically (and sometimes actually) shake their heads and ask themselves, 'Who is this stupid old fool and why is he boring us like this?'

It's my fault, I suppose, for always wildly misjudging the age gap. Because I feel no older and no different now than I did at eighteen, I tend to assume that anyone vaguely approximating to me in age and appearance must be a contemporary. It's a mistake any middle-aged man can be forgiven for making.

After all, in my parents' day, a forty-five-year-old was decidedly over the hill and he made no bones about it. He would rarely have had the opportunity to meet a member of the younger generation at close quarters and, if he did, he would doubtless have recoiled at the slightest hint of long hair or eccentric clothing. For us modern oldies, the hair, the jeans, the pot and the slang are something that many of us have been through ourselves. Are still going in some cases. And if we haven't or aren't, it is all sufficiently part of our sociological landscape that we do not fly into an apoplectic rage at the sight of a beard.

Indeed so youthful are we all these days that we think nothing of chucking up a marriage after twenty years and starting the whole process all over again. London parks today are stiff (no joke intended) with grey-haired men pushing fifty and their newborn babies along the paths, looking thoroughly relaxed about the whole thing. Their fathers, in similar situations, supposing they had lost their heads to the extent of begetting a second family, would probably have gone round heavily disguised with false moustaches and balaclava helmets. That is if they had dared go out of doors at all.

Occasionally, there are those middle-aged men who still do not find it easy in their hearts to approve of their friends and contemporaries launching into a frantic second parenthood when they feel they should really be declining into graceful grand-parenthood. Comments can range from the tactless 'Pretty grandchildren you've got' to the jovially offensive. 'Aren't you a bit past it, you silly old sod?' was the reaction a grey-haired friend of mine got from another man of his age upon learning that he was about to become a father for the second time in his mid-fifties. 'People can mock if they want,' he told me later. 'It's only envy.' He's quite right, of course. The middle-aged father inevitably has a huge age gap to close and the day is bound to come when my children are going to tumble to the fact that their father really *is* a silly old sod. In the meantime, however, they are going to enjoy an upbringing which is considerably more enlightened and benign than they could hope for from younger parents.

I say this with a degree of confidence that may surprise certain younger married couples of my acquaintance – and indeed, who knows, perhaps some of my own age too. But then, enjoying as I do the distinction unique amongst my circle of friends of having fathered two boys after the age of forty, I do speak from a position of some authority.

Anyway, it stands to reason that parents are more tender, more conciliatory and generally more understanding about their children at forty and fifty than they are at twenty and thirty. (I am talking now about very small children not teenagers, about whom I shall have some trenchant observations to make shortly.)

After all, the older one gets, the more cynical and the less idealistic one becomes both for oneself and for one's children. Younger parents are understandably competitive for their children; we who are older and wiser know that it is not always the children who do best at school who are also the most successful and happy in life. On the contrary. Expend all your energies on becoming a prefect or winning your school colours or carrying off the Greek Verse Prize and you won't have any left for the boardroom, the editorial conference or, indeed, the boudoir. Mark you, I wouldn't dare mention that to either of my sons' headmasters. I'd be far too frightened. (Does there ever come a time when one isn't, I wonder?)

I suppose I can't blame my friends for laughing at the thought of me staggering in last in the parents' egg and spoon and completely destroying my child's credibility with his chums in 5 B by dropping down with a coronary, bang in the middle of prize-giving. What they, and my sons, do not know is that I still retain a vivid memory of my own dear father's unfortunate performance in the parents' sack race at my kindergarten school when he was a mere lad of thirty-three, and when the cry goes out on the loud hailer for competitors in the fathers' egg and spoon, sack, obstacle or any other humiliating race to which the school sees fit to submit us, I shall suddenly find myself called away to an important, nay, unavoidable meeting.

Not only would I not wish to embarrass my children but, more importantly, I am not about to have them embarrassing me. Children can cut one unwittingly to the bone when thwarted in front of their friends, and shouts of, 'Daddy, why have you gone all red in the face?' and 'Daddy, why are you crawling along the ground like that?' are not guaranteed to boost one's already flagging moral or physique.

I thought the boy on my table at prep school who exclaimed in tones of horrified disbelief as I sat down to breakfast on the morning of Sports Day, 'Sir, surely not a blazer with *suede shoes!*' was exceptionally precocious. Now I'm not so sure that his comments were not an example of innocent honesty, if my two-and-a-half year-old's cries of 'Shut up, Daddy' and 'Silly fool, Daddy' right in the middle of my recitation of 'Oh where, oh where has my little dog gone?' are anything to go by.

He has already started weighing in with gratuitous *ad hominem* cracks of a most offensive nature. Only the other day he wrinkled his nose during *Play School* and announced, *à propos* nothing in particular, 'Daddy poofy pongy socks. Yucky.' The writing is definitely on the wall.

Nor am I naïve enough to believe that things are likely to improve with age. In the course of my researches I have carried out in-depth interviews with various middle-aged fathers with teenage children. All had me tottering away down the street, cold sweat starting out on my brow, asking myself if fatherhood, into which I had launched myself so recently and with such enthusiasm, was really for me after all.

I was struck by one in particular, which typified so many of the stories I was told: Malcolm. Age forty-five. Estate Agent. Married with two children – Morag, nineteen and Benedict, twenty.

'Things really started to get under way during their second year at comprehensive. Suddenly we began to be aware that they and a group of their friends, about fifteen strong, spent all their free time moving from house to house, making use of all the available facilities, which in our case meant the video machine, the telephone, the Badedas and so on, eating all the available food and finishing off the last bottle of milk that we had put aside for the cauliflower cheese we were planning for supper, before moving on, leaving us to come home to dirty crocks everywhere, coffee stains on the upholstery, spaghetti welded onto the cooker etc. If we happened to be in when the invasion began, the same sort of thing would go on except that it would all take place in one of their bedrooms. The noise was often unbearable, especially after we'd been in bed for an hour or so, but we never went in except for a very good reason indeed, e.g. the mouldings coming away from the ceiling – that sort of thing.

'By the time they were around fifteen and sixteen, things got really bad. Nothing about us was right. They never wanted to do what we did. I mean, for example, we'd suggest going for a walk and halfway they'd just sit down and refuse to go any farther. When we asked them why, they'd reply that they were bored. All their teachers at school were either neurotics, drunkards or sex maniacs. They even started laughing at the sort of clothes we wore, and yet there they were all going round in funny pointed shoes that I thought had gone out in 1958. When I made a comment to that effect, they said that shoes were the only way they had of expressing their individuality.

'They had to go punk, of course. All the old pop groups were out and defunct. They were just rip-off artists. Money-making wasn't everything. Anyone could be a star. Actually it was quite fun at first. Benedict went round with spiky blue hair saying that he was fed up at being ripped off by the record companies. We said that there was probably some truth in what he said. That annoyed him, of course. The more they could open up the generation gap, the happier they were. One day he gave it all up and took to classical music instead. Morag stuck at it longer. I don't think it was the philosophy behind it all that appealed to her so much as the gobbing. There was something about seeing a group like The Clash completely covered in spit that really cheered her up. That and the pogo-ing up in time to the music and elbowing people as you came down.

'Pot never seems to have worried them much. Or sex. Actually, Benedict's given up drinking and smoking and goes for early-morning runs and Christian meetings now. Morag has boyfriends but isn't interested in any regular relationships. None of that walking home hand-in-hand-after-the-cinema stuff. She hates discotheques. Discotheques to her are like the dogs are to a real racing man.

'Neither of them appears to have any ambitions. I did what I could to help Morag prepare for her 'O' Levels by testing her and suggesting ways of presenting her work. I even lent her my pocket tape recorder for making revision notes. After she'd failed, she said, "You were no help to me at all." She also broke my tape recorder. I don't know quite what she's going to do. At the moment, she helps out in a clothes shop in the King's Road on Saturday mornings.

'We don't communicate a lot with either of them nowadays. Occasionally we find notes on the kitchen table saying "No more Shreddies" and "More Club biscuits". But that's about it. They're around when they choose to be around. You know. Occasionally we have arguments about washing up all the dirty dishes they leave in the sink. But then they start on about how difficult life is for them, so we finish up doing it ourselves. Really they live exactly like young aristocrats in the nineteenth century. Everything is done for them and they contribute practically nothing. Even after we've washed their clothes for them in the machine they can't be bothered to take them out.

'I've come to the conclusion that children exploit their parents at any age. They're very hard, and we sometimes wonder whether it was all worth it. But at the same time we wouldn't have missed it all for anything.

'If only they wouldn't leave dirty mugs all over the house . . .'

Oh dear, oh dear . . . what have I let myself in for? Still whatever anyone may say I shall continue to dote upon the tiny apples of my eye and try to feel about twenty-eight and rather pleased with myself. I'll laugh off all those envious barbs such as 'Well, you've really made a rod to beat your own back with now, haven't you?' I'll try not to become too much of a bore; I've got enough on my plate as it is without the added burden of sleepless nights brought on by shaming memories of sharp put-downs. A middle-aged friend of mine is still traumatised by a remark made by his sister-in-law when he was waxing over-lyrical about his new offspring. 'We *do* love our little Bim,' he told her, his voice trembling with emotion. 'Yes,' she replied sharply. 'We're *all* very fond of our children.'

I realise that by the time William, now four months, is a teenager, I shall be fifty-five and that I shall be white-haired and distinguished when he is twenty-one and shall very likely attend the celebrations in a bath-chair. But then, of course, there are those who think one isn't even middle-aged until one reaches sixty. And besides, I'll be just the right age by then to interview all the new girlfriends.

Look at it this way. While my contemporaries slide remorselessly towards old age and devote their afternoons to oblivion in an armchair and their early evenings to the whisky decanter, I shall be reliving my childhood with *Winnie-the-Pooh* and *Jennings at School* and visits to the zoo and conkers on the common.

At the moment, we are heavily into *See-Saw*, and if anyone can tell me of a more pleasant way of passing that empty half an hour immediately after lunch than in front of the telly in the jovial company of Bod and Mr Benn, King Rollo and Bagpuss, Bric-a-Brac and Chockablock, I should be glad to hear of it. Indeed I think I would go so far as to claim to be one of the country's leading experts on the Life and Times of Postman Pat, so much so that I am seriously considering entering with it as a special subject on *Mastermind*.

Keeping up with the Young

I trust my enthusiasm for children's television does not smack too much of a conscious attempt to ingratiate myself with the young. There is no worse sight, in my view, than that of a middle-aged man trying to keep up with his children in dress, tastes and behaviour.

I have already made my views very clear on the subject of Last-Chance Trendies and their fondness for cheap and unsuitably tight clothing, and I shall have more to add later in my chapter on Sex and the Middle-Aged Man.

In the meantime, I should like to offer a word or two of advice to the born-again teenager on how not to make too much of an idiot of himself. (Or as the Americans would doubtless say, with their unerring eye for good taste and their obsession with bottoms, 'asshole'.)

Disco dancing: Way back in the fifties, when Ted Heath was only a band leader and record players were called gramophones, young men in their teens would be invited to things called dances where they would go up to young ladies and say, 'I wonder if you would care to have this dance,' whereupon, if their luck was in, and in those days it usually was, he would gather the object of his interest lightly in his arms and move around the floor to the strains of a small orchestra, using certain set steps which he had been taught at some expense during the holidays at what used to be known as a dancing class. The one I attended at the Hoskins Arms Hotel in Oxted was run by a lady in a pink angora sweater who owned a collection of Victor Sylvester 78s that today would earn her a place in *The Guinness Book of Records* and an interview on *Start the Week*, and two white poodle dogs whom she would get to stand on their hind legs and so help her to demonstrate the steps of the tango or the foxtrot. Being able to turn one's foot to any rhythm the band might strike up was considered in those days a considerable, even essential, social asset and could, if judiciously applied, assure one of entry into the very best circles. Even membership of the golf club.

Nifty female dancing partners were also much sought after and most girls' boarding schools would offer Ballroom Dancing as an optional extra. However, too much quickstepping with a member of one's own sex could lead to all sorts of unforeseen problems. The brother of a friend of mine was understandably nonplussed when, at his first dance, the young lady with whom he was doing his duty at the time suddenly, after several tours of the floor, clapped him vigorously on the back and announced, 'I'll be man now'.

Such scenes from provincial life are few and far between in these days of roller discos. In fact I can barely remember now what it felt like to lay one's arm across a broad expanse of taffeta with the words, 'Good band, isn't it?'

Not that I am quite so advanced in years that I have never known what it is like to step it lightly, unaccompanied, to the compelling beat of a bass guitar and a snare drum. I can always recognise my contemporaries at parties nowadays; they are the ones rolling around in an elephantine and extraordinarily simplified version of The Twist. As an ex-champion Twister, I tend not to perform myself nowadays any more than Fred Astaire probably sets off round the floor at the faintest hint of a foxtrot. It's not that I wouldn't wish to show up less twinkle-toed forty-year-olds so much as that . . . well, you know how it is . . . when you've been really good at something. . .

Not that I blame the poor old things their lumbering efforts. Not only was The Twist almost certainly the last dance they consciously learned to do; it was about the last one it was *possible* to learn.

There was an updated French version of the Hokey-Cokey called Le Madison that was all the rage in Alpine ski resorts in the early sixties, and there was all that athletic, freestyle, John Travolta stuff that everyone got so excited about a year or two ago; but on the whole, dancing has been very much a matter of improvised self-expression in the last twenty years. Either you looked good on a dance floor or you didn't, and most people of my age, through no fault of their own, just didn't and don't.

Happily, it is many a long year since I last set foot in what used to be known in my young day as a night club, and it is not a practice that I am likely to take up at my late stage in life. I have no interest in rubbing shoulders with football managers, faded pop stars, wholesale frock merchants from Great Portland Street, the brothers of landscape gardeners or Bubbles Harmsworth, or of rapping with forgotten names from the sixties, or of being served exorbitantly-priced cocktails by negro waiters in black silk shorts and T-shirts on roller skates. And neither, if they are wise, should anyone else of my age. As an up-and-coming young journalist who knows about these things said to me the other day, 'Nice people simply don't go to night clubs.'

Pop Music: An area of modern life in which more LCT's make bigger fools of themselves than in any other. However, before I go any further, I think I should preface my comments on the middle-aged man and the pop scene with a few remarks re my own position in the pop culture.

The sad truth of the matter is that, when it comes to popular music, I belong to the lost generation of forty-year-olds who were just too young for the sugary smoothness of the crooners and just too old for the noisy exuberance of the pop groups. Brought up as a schoolboy on a diet of Dickie Valentine, Guy Mitchell and Ronnie Hilton, with just the occasional injection of excitement from Edmundo Ross and his orchestra and Lonnie Donegan, the arrival on the musical scene of Bill Haley and his Comets drove me into a state of shock from which I did not really begin to recover until the early sixties. While others had their lives changed for ever by Elvis Presley, I retreated into the café world of Noël Coward and Hutch.

Certain tunes stand out in my memory from my university days of 61, 62 and 63: 'Twist Twist, Senora' by Gary (US) Bonds, 'Hit the Road Jack' by Ray Charles, 'Scotch and Soda' by the Kingston Trio, a song called 'Listen to the Rhythm of the Falling Rain', another called 'Walk Right In', 'A Picture of You' by Joe Brown and the Bruvvers, and the only song by Elvis Presley that ever registered with me, 'Can't Help Falling in Love'. Don't ask me why. I daresay there was a girl involved somewhere.

Thanks to a last minute panic over exams in the early 1963, early Beatles songs like 'Love Me Do' and 'From Me to You' barely impinged on my consciousness, and by the time Beatlemania had really started to get under way, I was in Switzerland teaching English and General Behaviour, at that girls' finishing school.

Being extremely susceptible at that age to all things French – Gauloises cigarettes, highly charged love affairs, intense conversations about existentialism, the *nouvelle vague* cinema and all the rest of it – I seemed to spend an inordinate proportion of my spare time prancing around in *boîtes de nuits* to the sounds of Johnny Halliday and Sylvie Vartan, smooching to Françoise Hardy, and congratulating myself on appreciating the Gallic wit and wisdom of Gilbert Becaud and Charles Aznavour.

And then one day a very extraordinary thing happened. It was announced that the Casino in Montreux was to host the British television pop programme *Ready Steady Go,* and anyone who wished to be part of the audience would be readily welcome. Though hardly my *tasse de thé*, I felt it only right that I should slope along and show the flag. It was all rather jolly and I was feeling justifiably self-satisfied that we British could always be relied upon to put on a decent show when necessary and vaguely toying with the idea of making myself known to Cathy McGowan, when on came what I can only describe as a bunch of loonies. There were five of them – three guitarists, a drummer and a singer who leapt about in a frenzied way, gesticulating wildly and pulling grotesque faces at the audience. It wasn't, as far as I recall, their behaviour that rendered me speechless with disbelief, or even their clothes, which were – by Swiss standards anyway – eccentric, but their hair. I mean, the Beatles' mops had been shocking enough but this shoulder-length stuff was, as one was to learn to say in later years, something else.

The cold hand of panic seized me by the vitals. Something, I told myself, has gone terribly wrong in England while I've been away and the sooner I leave this backwater of civilisation and offer such assistance as I can to fighting this epidemic of decadence, the better.

By way of strengthening my resolve, I made my way to the bar for a stiff Dubonnet. No sooner had I restored a little of my erstwhile southern European colour to my cheeks than who should come marching in than the five ginks in question, led by a small weasely looking man in glasses who settled his boys in a corner while he ordered a round of drinks at the bar. We soon got chatting about this and that. Quite why he took it into his head that I was a journalist, I can't imagine. All I know is that I must be one of the few people ever to carry out a full-length, in-depth interview with the Rolling Stones and never bother to publish a word.

They couldn't have been a friendlier bunch if they'd tried. I have a feeling Mick and I chatted about economics degrees, though I may have imagined it. At all events, I took great care to keep off the subject of their so-called music, confining myself to a pat on the back and the ironic remark, 'Ah well, lads, stick to it. I'm sure you'll do very well one day.'

The gingery man, who was called Andrew and was, it turned out, their manager, seemed delighted with the way the interview had gone. So was I when I got back to the finishing school and the

girls started throwing themselves at me in a frantic attempt to
touch the jacket whose shoulders had rubbed those of Mick,
Keith, Brian *et al*. I enjoyed my last few weeks at that school very
much indeed.

I vaguely thought of getting in touch with the Stones when I
returned to England, but somehow I never quite got round to it. A
pity really, because I was quite handy on the guitar myself in those
days . . . But all in all I'm glad things turned out the way they did,
for both our sakes. I don't think I'd have fitted very easily into the
world of late nights, marijuana and groupies. Frankly, although
only a year or two older than Mick, I was a bit past all that kind of
thing even then. Oh, I used to watch *Top of the Pops* with my
flatmates in the mid-sixties – Spencer Davis, The Animals, The
Kinks, The Dave Clark Five; but actually, it wasn't the music we
turned on for every week so much as the girls with their mini-
skirts. Oh, those mini-skirts . . . And do you remember hot
pants. . . ?

But enough of these menopausal musings. The point is that
once the skirts dropped, so did my interest in popular music, and I
really cannot pretend to have been anything of a follower of form
for at least fifteen years.

About eighteen months ago, I did take one trip down forget-me-
not lane when I agreed to accompany my wife to Earls Court to
see Bob Dylan in concert. The evening was not – even my wife
was bound to admit – altogether the unqualified success she had
been anticipating. In the circumstances I was very glad I did not
fall in with her suggestion that we dress for the occasion in jeans
and a cheesecloth shirt. Not only would I not wish to have
associated myself with all those hundreds of middle-aged trendies who seemed to make up such a large proportion of the
audience, but the weather that June was far from seasonal and I'd
have died of exposure just crossing the forecourt.

Frankly, whatever it was that Mr Dylan found to protest about
so strongly back in the sixties, it could hardly have begun to
compare with the parking problems one was asked to face in the
Earls Court area on that particular Monday evening. Or, for that
matter, his time-keeping.

Perhaps I am very old-fashioned, but to my way of thinking, £9
is an awful lot to pay out for the doubtful privilege of being kept
waiting, without any explanation whatever, for well over half an
hour, on a bullet-hard seat at parachute altitude, only to have my
ear bent by so-called performers I could hardly see I was so far

away, yelling incomprehensible things at me through loud-speakers. I can get all that any day of the week on British Rail. Having anticipated a mild little man, alone in a spotlight, with a guitar and a mouth organ attached to a piece of wire, singing plaintive airs about tambourine men, I was in for a very rude shock indeed.

As if my head was not humming enough already from the din issuing from the speakers, I had to put up with the couple in the seat next door smoking marijuana throughout the proceedings, so much so that after an hour I felt so dizzy and headachy that I had to leave.

Is it any wonder that I made no attempt to buy tickets either for the Rolling Stones on their recent tour of Britain, or even for those old favourites of mine, Simon and Garfunkel? Quite apart from the disappointment I should undoubtedly have suffered, the very fact of going to see them at all would have marked me out as an archetypal LCT who, when he is not trying to prove to himself that he was right after all (as in the case of Simon and Garfunkel), is waxing lyrical about music that he wouldn't have been seen dead listening to ten years ago (viz: the Rolling Stones).

Not that you can altogether blame him. After all, compared with today's Heavy Metal groups, Jagger enjoys all the respectability of an old cathedral amidst high-rise tower blocks.

Of course, there is always the LCT who will do anything to show he is up with the latest trends. He will scour the pages of *Time Out* for news of the latest gigs and hurry off to the darker reaches of Brixton and Westbourne Park to listen to groups with names like Buzzcocks, Pigbag, Dial-a-Coypu, and Attila the Stockbroker.

Chances are that he will reveal himself sooner or later for the silly old fool he really is – either by getting tight, (very much frowned upon by the younger generation nowadays) or by wearing bondage trousers and bumflaps and jumping up and down and gobbing (real punks gave all that up years ago); or worst of all by mentioning the Beatles (to which the response is likely to be, 'Oh yer, my Mum talks about them sometimes').

My advice to the middle-aged man who still enjoys pop music is: be yourself. If you suddenly realise that what really gets the old juices flowing is Barry Manilow, don't fight it. Minelli, Midler and Streisand live – and will continue to do so long after Adam Ant is back in the hole he popped out of in the first place. We oldies have had all the excitement we can take, thank you very much. The Clash are never going to be able to hold a candle to the Seekers, and it's no use pretending otherwise. As a friend of mine remarked once, *à propos* some particularly beastly modern group: 'It's like farting. Marvellous when you do it, but terrible when someone else does it.'

Motor cycling: I cannot really remember now what it was that finally persuaded me to buy my motorbike. Although not perhaps as thrusting and forceful a character as some I know of my age, I have never enjoyed travelling on public transport, especially in London. I think it is the smell that puts me off as much as the slowness and unpredictability of it all. Someone once remarked that walking into an underground train was like walking into someone's bad breath, and I have never really been able to do so since without automatically holding my breath for long periods at a time. This can prove tiring on journeys from Clapham South to Chancery Lane. As for buses, they have always smelt to me exactly like old ashtrays.

But my reasons for taking to two wheels were not altogether hygienic. Ever since I bought a second-hand Lambretta for £20 as an Oxford undergraduate and used to zip about here and there with earnest ladies from St Hugh's astride my pillion, I have always thought of motorcycling as a particularly romantic form of travel.

In 1966 I bought an even cheaper Vespa from a dealer in Brixton. I couldn't believe how quickly and easily I could travel from my flat near Baker Street to my office near Trafalgar Square. Indeed, I thought nothing at all of taking secretaries home for lunch – well, I did actually; it was they who never seemed quite as impressed as I'd hoped.

Not that anyone seemed exactly dumbstruck when I bought my Honda in 1974. I had seriously thought of following the example of the ex-editor of the *Sunday Times*, Mr Harold Evans, whom I had once spotted dressed from head to toe in expensive leathers, moving with a throaty roar (from his bike, not from him) through the traffic in Theobalds Road astride a huge BMW (motorbike, not car). But frankly, I never really felt I needed to prove anything to anyone, or indeed to myself. The C50, though not perhaps the sportiest of machines perhaps on the market, would, I decided, get me from point A to point B just as quickly and a good deal less expensively than any flashy-looking 900 cc job. Moreover, when the traffic was really impenetrable, I could always push it along the pavement. Happily, I have been proved correct in both particulars.

I think I was right not to waste a lot of money on a leather suit. In these liberal times, even the most innocent behaviour can all too easily be misinterpreted. Besides, the loose-fitting khaki ensemble, though not quite as dashing or indeed as waterproof as I might have wished, served its purpose excellently. I would still be wearing it today had the legs not come apart just outside Peter Jones. The bike itself was stolen from my front garden a couple of years ago to be replaced (by me, not the thief) by an equally reliable blue C50. The Honda sign fell off the other day, I don't know why.

Once or twice I have been the victim of that strange snobbery with which the motorcycling world is shot through. I remember once a secretary in a PR firm I was visiting showing great interest in the fact that I had come by motorbike, until she asked to see the machine. 'I thought you said you had a motorbike,' she said. I have also been mistaken by one or two receptionists for a messenger boy.

All in all, though, I cannot recommend motorcycling enough as a means of getting to and from work. The grey hairs one acquires from dicing with death with buses, container lorries and darting pedestrians may in the end outnumber those that go that colour while waiting for a 19 bus, but better a white-haired man of forty-three who gets to work on time with (if he's lucky) the sun on his face, the wind in his hair and fresh air in his lungs than a grey-haired mole on the verge of a coronary.

Mind you, motorcycling in a big city can ruin you for driving for ever (see Car, The Middle-Aged Man and his).

Sports cars: Another guaranteed way of giving yourself prematurely white hair is by buying a powerful sports car. It is noticeable that the only two types of men you see around town nowadays in Ferraris and Maseratis are either irritatingly young and good looking or else rather on the elderly side, with clenched white knuckles and hair to match. Both types tend to sport personal gold bullion, usually around the neck, and both wear the smug self-conscious look of teenagers who, without knowing quite how or why, have landed the prettiest girl at the party. They can't get over the fact that they've got her; the trouble is, they're not quite sure what to do with her.

This is, on the whole, truer of the LCT driver than of the

young, would-be stud. Having spent thirty years or more at the wheel of a Cortina, or at best, a TR4, the shock of finding himself in charge of a real 'performance vehicle' such as a Porsche or a Lamborghini is enough to turn anyone's hair white.

If the cost alone – around £30,000 a throw and a petrol consumption rate of about eight miles to the gallon – doesn't turn him into a Jock Ewing look-alike, driving the damned brute certainly will.

As the manager of a garage dealing in sporty cars explained to me, 'I won't mince words. A bloke who's never been behind the wheel of a Ferrari or a Lambo really ought to go out and have driving lessons. He's a fool to himself if he doesn't. Well, it stands to reason. Nought to sixty in seven seconds! Got to be joking. To start with, you've got to get your revs up if you want to get away smoothly. I had a customer, man in his fifties, never driven anything tastier than a Stag. (Not that I've got anything against Stags, mark you; beautiful piece of machinery; collector's item nowadays; perhaps I could interest you in one? No?) Anyway, bought a 250 LM Ferrari off me. Four new clutches in six months! Know why? Thought he could get away on 2–3,000 revs. Slipped his clutch like mad. Bingo. You've got to hold your revs at 1500 for at least a minute before your engine is even warmed up. Then of course he only ever drove the thing round town. What happens? Spark plugs snarl up, cylinders up the spout, never out of the garage.

'Poor old sod. Suppose he thought he was going to pull the birds. At that price he would have done better flying them to the South of France every weekend. It's pathetic really, middle age.'

Trends: Time was, back in the sixties, when it was just about possible for a man over forty to be a dedicated follower of fashion and get away with it. Unfortunately, far too many middle-aged men are still deluded into thinking that what was trendy in 1968 can still pass muster among the young fifteen years later. Hence the continual flowering of gaudily covered stomachs over tight-fitting waistbands and Indian silk scarves held at chubby throats by gold rings.

Still, anything is less cringe-making than the sight of an LCT sloping along the King's Road on a Saturday afternoon in his jeans and pedal pushers and baseball shoes, his grey Matt Curtis hair stuck out above his wrinkled forehead like a motorway flyover, hoping against hope that he will be accepted for Rocka-billy Night at the disco.

The fifties are over, James Dean is dead, OK, and Marlon Brando is an overweight sixty-year-old, and if you were too busy at the time doing your National Service with the RAF Osnabrück or out every night dancing with the likes of Suna Portman or worrying about The Bomb to be an angry young man, then that's just too bad. Nothing you can do about it now is going to bring back your youth.

In which I chart my increasing failure to cope with almost every aspect of social life – cocktail parties, dinner parties, christenings, weddings, funerals, and dining out in restaurants.

Chapter Eight

Cocktail parties

Writing to George Lyttleton in August 1956, Rupert Hart-Davies, then forty-eight, described a conversation he had had with his old friend Edmund Blunden.

'He will be sixty in November, and when I asked him the other day whether he didn't sometimes forget how old he was (as I do) and momentarily imagine himself young again, he said, "Yes, and when I was young I hoped that one day I should be able to go into a post office to buy a stamp without feeling nervous and shy; now I realise that I never shall." How lucky one is not to have been born with diffidence that must cause agony.'

How true. I know just what poor old Edmund must have gone through. I feel exactly the same way about social gatherings of all sorts. Show me a room full of people drinking and laughing and talking and generally giving every impression of enjoying themselves and I shrivel up like a salted snail, my mouth goes dry, my tongue and throat go into spasms, my brain suffers instant atrophy, sweat stands out on my brow and I wish I were dead.

Mark you, if I go on like this every time I have to go out for a drink I very soon will be. Which is why I have finally decided to cut down on parties and cocktail parties – from about one a year to one every five years.

As a young man, the prospect of a party never failed to set the blood coursing keenly through my veins. One never knows who one might not meet, I would tell myself. And indeed I very rarely met a single soul. I was Britain's first-ever male wallflower. Sometimes I would stand in a corner with a drink in my hand watching the proceedings with an air of amused interest; often I would settle into a chair with a good book and get through several chapters before calling it a day and heading for the door. Not only did this reading ploy give me something to do, but I had heard somewhere that nothing was guaranteed to attract women more than an air of detachment, and the thought that at any moment I might look up to find myself face to face with the most beautiful girl in the room was never far from my mind. Actually, it did happen once. The blood drained from my face and my heart felt as if at any moment it would come leaping out of my throat. 'Hallo,' I said. 'Hallo,' she said. 'I was just wondering. . .' 'Yes?' I said. 'You couldn't possibly be sitting on my handbag, could you?' she said.

Like Edmund Blunden, I never improved. In my mid-twenties I took to driving half across London to parties and standing on doorsteps for minutes on end listening to the sounds of revelry issuing from within, before finally turning tail and rushing for my car like a rabbit to its burrow.

The older I got, the worse I became. As a married man, I found myself dragged off willy-nilly to a number of drinks does. My wife, who, as a young slip of a thing, had been something of a regular on the social round, would greet old friends and chatter away about this and that while I would stand there, silent and smiling inanely, hoping against hope that if I continued to maintain a low profile, none of them would feel obliged to draw me into the general badinage. Most felt no such obligation and the few that did quickly began to wish they had let sleeping husbands lie.

My problem, you see, is that I have no small talk. This is a fact, not a boast. If someone asks me a question, I cannot, unlike the vast majority of those present at such occasions, resist the temptation to take it seriously. Naturally, I realise I've fallen for it again, as their smiles freeze on their lips and their eyes start to wander over my shoulder; but of course, to stop at that stage would be to make me seem even more foolish than I obviously am and so on I chunter, attempting occasionally to leaven the dough of my argument with the yeast of a literary allusion or a philo-sophical pleasantry, and always failing. Matters are not helped by the fact that when the noise level in a crowded room reaches a certain pitch I find I cannot hear what I am saying and, as a result, I open my mouth to say one thing and another comes out. To the listener, it must sound a bit like a snatch from a Pete Murray interview. I also, it goes without saying, cannot hear a word anyone is saying to me.

The net result is that my wife's old friends go away shaking their heads and saying how sad it is that she had to go and marry such an old bore, and so does my wife.

The worry is that she may well be right. If so, there is little I can do at this late stage in my life to improve matters. The more boring I become, the less we are invited out, and the less we move in society, the fewer the opportunities I am afforded to develop the gay persiflage so essential to one who wishes to be considered a social success.

Frankly, I have little further light to shine on this particular subject, and any middle-aged Edmund Blundens who have rushed eagerly to this chapter in the hope that I will be able to offer a solution to their social handicaps must, I am afraid, prepare themselves for disappointment.

However, here is a very fragile straw that the really desperate may care to clutch at if they feel so inclined. If, like me, you do not wish, through your own incompetence, to make your wife feel like a social pariah, then accompany her to the party, and the moment you are confident that she is happily engaged in conversation, make a mumbled excuse and slip away to the car or the nearest pub, returning an hour or so later to announce cheerfully that you hate to drag her away but it really is time you started making a move. She will assume that all this time you have been mingling and generally showing the flag and everyone will leave satisfied that they have done their duty. Only you need ever know the truth. I recently spent a very satisfactory hour with old Giles cartoons in a loo in a house in Holland Park during a large cocktail party while my wife performed sterling deeds of conversational derring-do and I do not believe either of us have enjoyed ourselves more. I'm only sorry it was the only loo in the house. Still, one must expect to pay for one's pleasures in this life.

Giving a party is marginally more tolerable than going to one, if only because one can, under the guise of being the perfect host and moving constantly among the guests offering top-ups and canapés, avoid any form of conversation whatever.

Even so, the very fact that all those people, most of whom one barely knows, are there in one's house at all, filling the place with noise and smoke, stubbing out their fag ends on anything that comes to hand or foot, from the avocado dip to the Wilton, and leaving alcoholic stains of every imaginable shape and size in the most unimaginable places, is enough to make one roll up one's sleeves and start chucking them out like the money changers from the temple.

P.G. Wodehouse had the right idea. His wife Ethel was a keen party thrower and their home often rang to the merry sound of laughter and chinking glasses. Not that it disturbed the great man. He was up in his room, rattling away at his typewriter keys.

Occasionally, however, he was ordered downstairs to play host, a role which he saw rather differently from most. His biographer, Frances Donaldson, describes turning up to a Wodehouse bash in London before the war, accompanied by her father, the playwright Frederick Lonsdale. They were surprised to be met on the doorstep, not by the butler, but by Wodehouse himself, beseeching them, 'Don't come in. Don't come in. You'll hate it.'

The Dinner Party

Always a tricky one this. Since basically the object of the exercise when you get to my age is to be at home and in bed before midnight at the very latest, one's chances of pulling this off depend to a very considerable extent on the time one actually sits down to table.

The Sri Lankans, if I may be allowed to name-drop for a moment, make life comparatively easy by kicking off with a fairly long drinking session, then sitting down to eat quite late, but shoving off home almost as soon as the last mouthful has disappeared down the hatch.

The English, on the other hand, start with a long drinking session, follow it up with a long eating session, followed by an even longer drinking session which lasts until guests or hosts or both agree to call it a day, or more strictly a night.

Beware of actors, especially if you are the host; they're the devil to get rid of after dinner and will stay until all hours working their way through your litres of Carafino like geologists in the southern Sahara. The trouble is, if they're out of work, which they usually are, they have nothing to get up for the following morning.

Neither, unfortunately, do the large majority of one's fellow dinner guests, employed or otherwise. I, on the other hand, do, and far from not knowing when to leave, experience no difficulty whatever in rising to my feet shortly after 11.30 with the words, 'Well, it's past our bedtime. We must be on our way.'

I must admit it is unfortunate that on occasions I have felt compelled to use these somewhat brusque tactics while still seated at table, but better that than to be still on the premises going through the rigmarole of coffee and blue jokes over the brandy while the ladies retire to powder their noses at one o'clock in the morning. Perhaps I am getting old, but there it is.

Still, I'm glad to say that I am not the only one of my age group whose thinking is along the same lines as mine. Only the other day we were rung up by a friend inviting us to dine with him and his wife in Islington. Having explained how to get there and at what time he added, 'By the way, I hope you don't mind, but we like our guests to leave by 11.30. I simply can't face setting off to work exhausted the following morning.'

Now there's a man after my own heart. I'd like to think that he might have set a real fashion for the over-forties.

Mind you, it is possible to carry this early departure habit too far. Some friends of mine were once asked to dinner by neighbours with whom they had little in common. They had even less with their fellow guests. They had also forgotten to come out with a watch between them. However, they did their best, battling valiantly with the conversation and the food for what they considered to be a more than suitable length of time. Finally, after coffee, they decided enough was enough, and after much heavy yawning and excuses about getting the babysitter home and 'past our bedtime', they made their adieux and arrived home to find it was only 9.30.

Christenings, weddings and funerals

Any social event at which the guests are liable to be reminded of the passing of the years and their own mortality should be given a wide berth by the middle aged whenever possible. Ditto events for which one is obliged to hire special clothing and in the process be reminded yet again of the gathering of the inches.

Naturally, if one is personally involved, as son, parent, grandparent or participant, these sort of affairs are rather difficult to skate out of, and naturally I wouldn't wish to appear a killjoy, but in my experience things like this nearly always end in tears or indigestion or both. And of course if one happens to be a member of the family involved, chances are that sooner or later some aged relative is going to tell you how terrible you look.

Restaurants

While maturity obviously brings with it a number of in-built benefits when it comes to dining out, it also has its serious drawbacks.

On the one hand, one knows, or at least one should know, how to read a menu in French or Italian without having to beckon the waiter and mutter, 'Er, exactly what is the Sole Wah-loos-ka?' One has the confidence to throw one's eye in a casual way over the wine list in the grandest joint, look the wine waiter straight in the eye and say, 'I think a carafe of your house red will more than meet the bill.' And when that bill comes, one knows how to look it over without (a) registering stunned disbelief and (b) looking as though one's checking on the head waiter's arithmetic. One also knows how to complain as well as how to compliment, and one has perfected that skill, so essential when dining with a lady who is not one's wife, of enjoying one's food without ever actually letting one's attention wander from her for a single second.

Now, of course, most of this know-how is quite irrelevant in the case of the business lunch, and for most middle-aged men, the only time they get to see the inside of the Ritz Restaurant or Inigo Jones is when someone's company is paying, preferably the other chap's. Either way, nobody's too fussy about what they eat, as long as it's something they don't usually get at home, like tournedos or lobster, or what they drink as long as it's expensive and has a date attached to it. The bill rarely rates more than the briefest glance before the plastic money is slapped down on top of it, and on leaving it is traditional for both business host and business guest to remove the Romeo y Julieta from between the teeth, flash the head waiter a squiffy smile and possibly an extra fiver, and say, 'Very nice indeed, thank you'. Everyone knows the form.

Social occasions, on the other hand, can rarely be treated with such insouciance. Not only are one's conversational skills stretched to their limits, especially when one suddenly finds oneself face to face with one's wife over the grissini and mineral water, but the long silences that ensue merely serve to remind one that one could be eating much better food for a quarter the price at home in front of the telly. And one wouldn't be up half the night with indigestion.

In which I examine the role of the middle-aged man *en famille* – his occasional triumphs and his frequent disasters – as DIY expert, gardener, family chauffeur, Father Christmas, au pair bait and television viewer.

Chapter Nine

Do-It-Yourself

One day last summer, I and my whole family were invited out to tea with some people who had recently moved into a house three or four streets away in Balham.

I had known her for years. She was a childhood friend of the man I shared a flat with when I first came to London in 1964 and we had seen a fair amount of each other over the years, as people unencumbered by spouses, children and other trappings of domestic life are wont to do. On a chummy basis, you understand; nothing serious.

And so it might have gone on indefinitely. But one of us had to crack one day and in the event it was she who went first – to a house in Battersea and a very nice actor and two children.

I didn't see a lot of her after that. Middle-aged bachelors do not fit easily into the fraught, noisy, untidy world of small children and trainee nannies and food all over the floor and conversation consisting almost exclusively of discussion about bowel movements.

And then finally, at the age of forty, I too succumbed to family life. News of my change of circumstance gradually filtered through to all my old friends, for in the spring of last year we received a card from them informing us that we were soon to be neighbours.

This apparently mundane piece of information was received in the Matthew household with scenes of mild jubilation. The prospect of new friends for the children to play with is, for parents of our age anyway, always pleasing and within a very short while of their moving in, a small caravan of prams and push-chairs, loaded with bibs and bottles, was on its way up Endlesham Road, heading north for the newly discovered pastures of Roseneath Road and Ballingdon Road.

Barely had we set foot in their beautifully fitted kitchen and admired their corner cupboard carousel and the blue dragged paintwork when we learned that owing to a mysterious leak in one of the hot-water pipes, the entire quarry-tiled floor which had been so lovingly laid and carefully sealed only a few weeks previously, would have to be completely ripped up, the trouble located and the whole thing started all over again.

Time was when domestic tragedies of this sort would have earned nothing more from me that a few muttered words of consolation, so eager would I have been to get on to the important issues of the day – had Jonathan Miller *really* retired from the theatre? How *did* one account for the success of the *Noël Coward Diaries*? What about *Smiley's People*?

But that was in another existence. These days, the description of how they persuaded the builders to convert the double doors from the sitting room into fitted cupboards in the main bedroom, the revelation that if you want planning permission for a loft conversion you have to fireproof all the upstairs doors first, and the news that there's a shop in Walton Street that does wonderful tiles for as little as 12½p each, is all very much grist to this home-owner's mill.

Now I don't want you to get the wrong idea. I am no handyman. The power jig saw and the twelve-inch claw hammer are virtual strangers to these thinker's hands of mine. On the other hand, I have been known to grout the odd bathroom tile before now, and I have insulated more than one draughty window. Men of my age are expected to be able to turn their hands to such things – unless of course they are very rich indeed, in which case the section that follows is of no interest whatever and they would be advised to move on to the section on vasectomy.

Now, of course, the middle-aged man who has spent a lifetime doing-it-himself, whether through dint of poverty or a genuine fondness for handicraft, will by now be asking himself what I am making such a song and dance about. Tacking up a strip of draught-excluder and mixing up some powder is for a DIY man of experience about as complicated and satisfying as coughing.

For someone like myself, who has come to house upkeep rather later in life than most, merely to change a washer is the equivalent of winning the Booker Prize for Literature. And it is for my fellow late developers that the following account of my experiences with screwdriver and bradawl is chiefly intended.

Actually, I may try to give the impression that I am totally incapable of doing anything myself, but the fact is that all husbands are to some extent DIY men.

From the moment one makes one's first tentative offer for a house or flat, scarcely a day passes but one is not chasing up one's solicitor, chivvying the builder, and chatting up the bank manager, every one of whom is charging one an arm and a leg for the privilege of one's own time, patience and negotiating skills.

So, too, are the removal men, whose every move (no joke intended) one is obliged to duplicate – although why one bothers I can't imagine since they are just as capable of putting the wrong piece of furniture in the wrong room as the customer.

Mind you, we were luckier than most. Our house was actually habitable when we moved in. Not for us the unplastered, bare walls, the open-plan floor joists, the ceilings hung with bare wires, the skip outside the front door. We had visited enough friends who seemed to live permanently in a camp site surrounded by a building site to know that at heart we were redecorators rather than restructurers.

Thus, although not a single interior wall was knocked through and not a single bathroom ensuited, we wasted little time tearing off the heavily flowered, quasi-Victorian wallpaper and replacing it with something that would give our place more the feel of a rather good English country house than a down-at-heel French brothel. Cheerful simplicity with a hint of elegance was to be the keynote.

I wish I could honestly claim that the subtle papers and delicate emulsions that now grace our walls were the work of my hand and my hand alone, but frankly, I have always felt that such talent as I possess for DIY lies less in the drudgery of stripping and filling and papering than in the detailed draftsmanship of picture hanging, curtain rail fixing and shelf construction.

What I had not realised, however, despite the gloomy reference by our little man to the 'naughty walls', was that in houses as old as ours, it is very much touch and go whether a given point into which one is planning to insert a rawlplug is going to be like half a pound of self-raising flour or the north face of the Eiger. As a result, a simple task, such as putting up a brass curtain rail in the drawing room, assumes all the thrill and uncertainty of roulette.

Take the case of the shelves. My wife favoured fitted shelves, but then the estimate arrived and I suddenly remembered that a more rustic, open-plan effect consisting of a few lengths of plain wood, held in place by aluminium supports, was really what I had in mind all along. And, let's face it, a man who is incapable of knocking up a dozen of those on either side of the fireplace in a morning really forfeits the right to call himself a husband and a father.

Quite why it had not occurred to me that in old houses there is not a floor, wall or ceiling that is blessed with a straight line I cannot think, but it hadn't. All I can tell you is that, despite my carefully calculated measurements, not a single shelf came within an inch of fitting inside the recesses.

Still, these electric saws one sees advertised on TV aren't *that* expensive or indeed difficult to use. The real problems come with the screws that hold up the six-foot aluminium strips into which the shelf supports fit. All thirty-two of them.

The point is, anyone can hold a strip up against the wall and make marks through the appropriate holes with a pencil, but drilling those holes in anything resembling a straight line is another matter altogether. To wit, the tightness of 90 per cent of the screws, the blood, the toil, the tears, the sweat, the bad language, the gouges, four banana-shaped aluminium strips, twelve extremely wobbly shelves, and serious talk of divorce.

Hilaire Belloc had the right idea and his words should be pinned up in the toolshed of every reasonably well-heeled house-holder who feels that slightest urge to do it himself:

Lord Finchley tried to mend the Electric Light
Himself. It struck him dead: and serve him right.
It is the business of the wealthy man.
To give employment to the artisan.

The Garden

It had always been one of my great ambitions in life to own a garden. I have somehow felt that it is every Englishman's God-given right to be able to sit in a deckchair on his lawn on a warm summer's afternoon, watching the bees doing their stuff on the herbaceous border, contemplating the broad beans, and vaguely thinking in terms of a little gentle snailing after tea.

If I had any picture in my mind of what sort of garden I hoped would one day be mine it was probably the one at Sissinghurst Castle. Like Harold and Vita, I too would create a famous garden out of a wilderness, and plant a nut walk and a white garden and charming vistas and little corners that were formal and yet at the same time natural. And in the evenings I would retire to a room in the tower and write respectable books, and in years to come, hacks would come down from the Sunday colour supplements and write articles saying that my garden was every bit as important a work of art as my novels, and Peter Coats would be commissioned to do a coffee table book about it with wonderful photographs and an elegant, admiring text.

In the event, the garden that came with our house in Balham was not quite Sissinghurst. It being only slightly larger than the average London drawing room, plans for a nut walk have had to be shelved for the time being. Ditto a formal rose garden. In fact, given a lawn, surrounded by a narrow strip of earth, one's scope for landscaping is to a certain extent limited, especially when every square inch of the earth is jammed solid with huge shrubs which loom at you from all sides and threaten, if not held at bay with saw and machete, to pounce on you as you pass and pull you among the roots and eat you.

Even so, I like to think that I have adapted it to my own very special tastes and moods.

It was a shame the snails had to go and eat the African Marigolds within a week of my bringing them home from the garden centre. And I am still kicking myself for not cutting back the honeysuckle sooner. The builder tells me that part of the roof can be replaced without too much expense. On the other hand, the pot of hanging geraniums on top of the wooden bird bath just outside the front door was little less than a stroke of genius (my wife still insists it was her idea), setting the tone, as it were, and preparing one for the pinks and reds and greens that greet one as one enters the house and looks out into the garden proper. Actually, strictly speaking, one is greeted by a wall covered with a large cracked mirror, and you have to turn right into the drawing room before you see the garden, but I have ideas for changing all that.

As for the pink rambler that nestles against the wall of the patio . . . well, if that doesn't make one believe one could be standing beside the South Cottage at Sissinghurst, I don't know what will. I'm only sorry I forgot to water it during that hot spell of weather in September. I think it'll pull through, though.

I would be exaggerating if I said that the garden occupied all my spare time, or indeed all my spare money. (I have thought from time to time of taking on a gardener, but it does one good to get close to the soil from time to time, and actually I quite enjoy cutting the edges, even if it does play my back up sometimes.)

On the other hand, I can see what middle-aged friends of mine mean when they talk of their gardens being a burden. It isn't just the fact that I now find I have to kneel down to weed, preferably on a foam rubber mat; after all, I can always follow the example of my father's next-door neighbour who, at the age of fifty, took to hoeing while sitting in a deckchair sipping a gin and tonic. No, it's worrying about the havoc that can all too easily be wrought upon it at any moment by the rest of my family.

Until now I had always been rather tickled by stories of how jealously gardeners guard their gardens, to the extent that owners are obliged to ask permission before cutting the zinnias and picking the runner beans. Now they have my total sympathy. The instant a single flower pops its head shyly above the undergrowth my wife is out there, scissors poised to cut the wretched thing down in its prime and leave it to wither in a vase on the dining room table.

Such blooms as have had the good fortune to escape her itchy fingers and the snails are doomed anyway to be leapt upon by the Kerry Blue terrier in its frantic efforts to get at the cats that taunt her hourly from the top of the wooden fencing, or stamped into the ground by my elder son for no apparent reason.

Shall I ever live long enough to see my dream fulfilled?

A middle-aged friend of mine recently gave up his country cottage because of the garden. What upset him was not the fact that he had to devote every spare second of every weekend to working in it, but that he had never once been able to enjoy the fruits of his labours. In the gathering dusk of Sunday evening he would lock his tools away in the shed, having brought his patch to a peak of perfection, pack his family into the car and head back to the city to return on the Friday evening in time to start all over again.

As a way of reminding ourselves of the transience of human

endeavour and of the speed with which the sand is dropping through the little hole in the hour-glass, the garden has few equals.

As you can see, I have little useful advice to offer on this subject. Still, it may be of some comfort to know that, in this, as in other domestic matters, you are not alone.

The Car

Now I'll have to be a bit careful writing this section because I could easily give myself a nasty turn just thinking about cars and garage bills and MOT tests and knock-for-knock insurance claims and loading up to go away for the weekend and traffic jams and Leytonstone High Street on a Saturday morning and the Exeter bypass – or do I mean the M56?

Is it really possible that I once actually enjoyed owning a car? Did I positively look forward to packing up my old Triumph Herald convertible on a warm Friday evening in the height of summer, letting down the roof and biffing off up the Hendon Way towards Apex Corner, the A1, Newmarket and the north Norfolk coast?

Could I really have derived a deep personal satisfaction from patching up the disintegrating wing with Isopon and chicken wire? And reboring an Austin Seven? And was it really possible that I once bought a car for £15, drove it, brakeless, at an average speed of 25 mph from West Sussex to East Anglia where I paid a man £1 to come and take it away? Indeed, was it actually legal? And am I dreaming or do I distinctly remember a colleague of mine at a prep school where I was teaching Latin in 1958 deciding he wanted to turn his old Hillman into a convertible and taking a hacksaw and literally chopping the top off? And did it really seem a jolly wheeze to spend fourteen hours on the trot in a Triumph Spitfire hammering down the N7 to the Riviera one August 1st along with the entire population of Paris?

It seems only yesterday that I looked upon motoring as an amusing, even romantic, pastime. What went wrong? Where is it fled the glory and the dream?

The answer, I suppose, is that what went wrong is that I grew older and tireder and less tolerant and more impatient behind the wheel. And as for that romantic vision of the open road with the wind in one's face and the old cylinders humming cheerfully as one bowled through the English countryside, all that dissolved into a morass of roadworks, traffic jams, articulated lorries and a general desire on the part of the vast majority of one's fellow motorists to kill anyone who so much as dares to overtake, push in front at a crossroads, or in any other way attempts to assert his superiority.

It also, in my case, disappeared in that quaint English domestic custom known as Packing up the Car to go on Holiday.

One of the greatest agonies the middle-aged man with a young family can suffer is that of knowing, from many long years of experience, how to carry out certain manoeuvres with the maximum efficiency and the minimum expenditure of nervous energy, but never being able to put this into effect. On no other occasion is this sub-section of Sod's Law seen to work to better advantage than on a long car journey.

You see, I happen to know beyond a shadow of a doubt that if one wishes to stand an earthly of getting from Balham to the Suffolk coast in under three hours in the summer months, it is absolutely vital that one leaves either after nine o'clock at night or before six thirty in the morning. Mistime your departure by a few minutes, which you're more or less bound to do, however scrupulously you prepare for it in advance, and you're in real trouble.

First of all, you'll get caught up with all those container lorries in the Lea Bridge Road and, if that happens, you can reckon on an hour and a half minimum to Brentwood. And what with that single-lane business just as you hit the dual carriageway and that nightmare of a roundabout at Chelmsford, you'll be lucky to be on the outskirts of Ipswich in under two and a quarter hours. Whereas of course you've really got to be passing the turnoff to Colchester at the one and three quarter mark if you're really going to stand a chance.

Now, you *can* slip through the centre of Ipswich instead of taking the ring road, but unless you hit that traffic light after the bus station just right, you could easily lose on the swings what you might have gained on the roundabout, and with the baby now showing signs of squawking and the toddler deciding he wants to go whizzer and the dog beginning to swallow in a deeply ominous way, you could well find yourself wishing you hadn't tried to be such a clever clog. And, of course, even when you've got through that little lot, you're still faced with that endless drag through Martlesham, usually behind a convoy of container lorries and elderly drivers in impeccable twenty-five-year-old Austin Cambridges who shouldn't really be allowed on the road at all, and before you know what, you're well over the three-hour mark and you still haven't got to Little Glemham. And talking about Little Glemham, why on earth they don't widen that stretch of the A12 between the end of the dual carriageway and the Aldeburgh turnoff I shall never understand; or at least ban it to all caravans except from one o'clock till four o'clock in the morning. There's only that one short stretch where it's possible to overtake and there's always something coming the other way. And why the dog always has to choose that moment to be sick. It's only a few miles further to go. I mean you'd think she could hold on for another fifteen minutes, wouldn't you, but oh no. . .

Hang on. Hold it. Now, there you are, you see. I had a feeling I might start throwing a wobbly if I went ahead with this stretch of the book, and I was quite right. If you don't mind, I think I'd better change the subject before the headache really starts up in earnest.

You know, the older I get, the more I find myself wondering if there isn't more to those Jimmy Savile advertisements than meets the eye. His hair may be white, but there's no getting away from the fact that he's looking very good for his age. People like that are not quite as daft as they look.

Parents, or You Make me Feel so Young

Bill Tidy has raised a few chuckles from me over the years, but of all his splendid cartoons, there is one that I cherish with special fondness. It depicts a number of what we have now learned to call task-force commanders standing round a table on which is a map covered with flags and arrows indicating various troop deployments. In charge of operations is a chunky-looking brigadier in bristling moustache and shirt-sleeve order, smacking a cane against one hand and barking, 'Now then, what would Nanny have done?'

I never had a nanny myself, but I did have a mother. Still do, I'm happy to say. And although at the age of forty-three I am rarely in the habit, when called upon to make life and death decisions, of wondering how my dear old mama would cope in similar circumstances I feel sure she'd hope that the thought might at least cross my mind.

Nor do I suppose for a moment that she is alone in so assuming. A man may be physically well into middle age, with children, possibly even grandchildren, of his own and yet mentally he never quite succeeds in catching up with his parents. No matter how rich and successful and fat and bald he has become, in their eyes he is to them, and always will be, a small boy.

Time was when I felt sure that it all had to do with whether one was married or not. As long as one was single (and I was single longer than most), one was fair game, and the moment one married, one's mother had more important things to worry about, such as whether the wife ironed as good a shirt as her son deserved. In fact, so much did I take this state of affairs for granted that never once did it strike me as odd that a mother should be ticking her thirty-five-year-old son off for not getting his hair cut before coming home for the weekend.

A friend of mine, an even older bachelor than myself and one who was doing rather well for himself in the City, was habitually treated with even scanter respect to his age and position. One weekend he arrived home in an obviously distressed state of mind. By dint of genial bludgeoning, his father, an ex-Army man, managed to extract from him the news that he had, earlier that evening, surprised his flatmate in his bed with a girl. His father was deeply shocked and announced that in the circumstances he felt it only right and proper that the two of them should travel back up to town and sort the matter out forthwith. He strode purposefully towards the door, then paused. 'First things first, though,' he said. 'We must get your mother to look you out some clean sheets.'

Nothing, it seems, is proof against the high-handed behaviour dished out by parents to their comparatively elderly children. I heard of a couple in their late thirties who, when visiting his parents, were always firmly placed in separate rooms, even when she was eight months pregnant; and of a woman of ninety-four who, when advised by her accountant to start handing some of her money over to her spinster daughter, snorted, 'I couldn't possibly think of such a thing. She is a mere child.' Her daughter was seventy-two at the time.

Marriage puts parents off their stroke a little but not completely. The old adage to the effect that the child is father to the man (or woman) applies almost as much to the forty-three-year-old with three children as it does to the callowest teenager. Only the other day, as I was leaving my parents' house for dinner with friends, I could have sworn I heard my mother asking me if I had a clean handkerchief.

Parents-in-law

Similar form, in my experience. Even after three years of marriage my father-in-law still enquires of my wife whether I am capable of supporting her.

I daresay it's my fault for insisting on addressing him, not by his Christian name in a no-nonsense, man-to-man way, but as 'Sir', like a schoolboy to his headmaster.

Mind you, had I perhaps broached the subject earlier in the proceedings, like Sir John Betjeman, I might have received some sort of parental-in-law guidance in the matter. The apocryphal story goes that upon becoming engaged, he enquired of his prospective father-in-law, Field-Marshal Lord Chetwode, how he should address him. Lord Chetwode thought for a moment and then said, 'I think Field-Marshal should cover it.'

Christmas

I have nothing further to add to what every middle-aged paterfamilias already knows only too well, viz: that Christmas is, without exception, the most expensive, the longest-drawn-out and the most physically and mentally exhausting family celebration of the whole year. It is also the most emotionally harrowing and the one during the course of which many find themselves seriously reassessing the suitability of their marriage partners and looking into the feasibility of a quickie divorce in Reno, Nevada, over the New Year holiday.

The build-up to Christmas begins some time in August, often on some sun-kissed Mediterranean beach, when the wife, *à propos* nothing in particular, casually utters the fateful words, 'What are we doing for Christmas then?'

What she means of course is: Whose parents are we going to be having to stay this year, or are we going to try to please everyone as usual and spend most of the holiday thumping up and down various foggy and frozen motorways?

At all events, any romantic Yuletide visions I may have been harbouring over the years of myself in middle age, dozing in front of a blazing log fire, paper hat on head and detective novel on chest, breaking off occasionally to carve a bird or hang a few glass balls, have long since vanished, to be replaced by altogether more realistic images of debilitating visits to the supermarket, mind-taxing discussions about who's made the Christmas card list and who's out, present-buying that starts in a relaxed sort of way at about the end of September and continues unabated until the very last panic-stricken dash to Marks & Spencer and W. H. Smith at five o'clock on Christmas Eve, and an outpouring of money from one's bank that makes the breaching of the Mohne Dam look like a tiny drip from a slightly cracked car radiator – all of which culminates, for me at least, in a day of over-excitement, over-indulgence, over-tiredness, of crumpled wrapping paper, discarded toys, tears, too much television and a drawerful of handkerchiefs I never use, socks that are the wrong size and bath gel which might well re-invigorate me were it not for the fact that I always use a shower.

But who am I to complain? My days of Christmas fun are long past. Christmas is a time for children not for middle-aged men. It's the innocent excitement in the faces of the young that makes Christmas the very special time of the year it is, not the pained, dyspeptic expression of the oldies. Our job is not to enjoy ourselves but to ensure the joy for our loved ones. If we wake at three o'clock on Christmas morning, it is not to see if Father Christmas has done his stuff, as per requests up the chimney, but to worry about all those cheques we've been scattering like snowflakes among the local shopkeepers.

In which case, is there any point in our being there at all on the day? Would it not be better for all concerned if, after decorating the tree, donning the Father Christmas outfit and doing the rounds of the bedrooms, one were to remove the hood and whiskers, put the cat out, toast oneself in a large whisky and soda, wish the sleeping figure of the wife a Happy Christmas, pack a small suitcase and steal off to Monte Carlo for a few days' well-earned rest alone in a large hotel suite with nothing to disturb one but the occasional discreet knock on the door from Room Service?

But, of course, this is a rhetorical question, and anyway there are no flights anywhere at that time of night.

However, while I am in Christmas vein, may I take this opportunity to point out on behalf of all ageing fathers that, should wives and offspring be considering the possibility of showing their appreciation for our kindness and generosity and selfless attempts to keep the whole thing going from one year's end to the next, there are ways of doing so other than in shirts, after-shave lotion and Wills Whiffs. The notion that the middle-aged man has lost all interest in unusual and imaginative gifts is out of date and downright unfair.

Why, for instance, is it only children who are given things like electronic games and Sony Walkmen? I long for the day when someone will give me a mini Space Invader machine that doubles as an alarm clock and calculator for doing the VAT. It would keep me happy for hours on end and leave the television set completely free for anyone who wanted to see *White Christmas* and the special seasonal edition of *To the Manor Born*. And I can imagine no nicer way of blotting out the yells of over-excitement and over-tiredness than by blowing my mind with the inimitable sound of Carroll Gibbons and his Savoy Orpheans.

The Au Pair Girl

Time was when the middle-aged, middle-class husband tradi-tionally knocked off the au pair, or if he didn't, someone else did. Either way, the girl would sooner or later be sent packing back to Germany or Denmark with the price of a one-way ticket in her pocket and a small bulge beneath her jeans. Indeed, so integral a part was it of middle-class folklore that when, after a month or two of our first au pair girl occupying the small room with the sloping roof at the top of the house, I was still quite unable to see anything more in her than the monosyllabic, largely unsmiling teenager that we had collected off the train at Victoria station, I began to harbour serious doubts about my sex drive. I didn't feel the slightest twinge of jealousy over the young man with the frizzy hair and denim jacket she used to bring home with monotonous regularity to eat our frozen pizzas and watch films on our video machine when we went out to dinner or the theatre, and often when we didn't. Occasionally it would strike me as odd that there I was, laying a fire for them in the sitting room while they lounged back watching *Top of the Pops* and my wife was out in the kitchen in her dressing gown and curlers ten minutes before we were due for dinner in Chiswick, cooking them a three-course meal; but I didn't like to say anything. Well, one doesn't as the man of the house, does one? One's wife is responsible for that side of things and let's face it, au pairs are meant to be part of the family, as it were. I mean they're not strictly speaking employees, and the £15 a week one gives them *is* only pocket money. A real trained nanny wouldn't look at you for under £100 a week and a colour telly in her room. All right, so one hears about people who don't think twice about working their au pairs into the ground for £15, but either they're not used to staff or else they're foreign, and really one wouldn't want a girl to go back to Scandinavia with a bad impression of the English way of life, would one? Besides, as I say, it *is* up to the wife to deal with things, isn't it?

To which the answer is yes, except that wives have an even more complicated love-hate relationship with au pair girls than husbands do, and while it is perfectly permissible for them to throw the occasional fit when it is suddenly revealed halfway through tea that the wretched girl has forgotten to wash the children's hands after an afternoon spent in the local playground, the husband is expected to speak his mind only in the case of the more serious misdemeanours and even then only when specifically requested to do so.

More often than not, one gears oneself up to read the Riot Act only to discover that one's wife has gone off the boil altogether and is wondering if instead you wouldn't mind running the girl and her friend from Clapham Junction up to their evening class since it took her rather longer to wash her hair than she had anticipated. All very frustrating for the poor husband who has just come in after a busy day at the office and is in the process of psyching himself up for the dreaded encounter with a whisky and soda or three. However, discretion is often the better part of valour on these occasions. Au pairs are a subversive lot, and it only takes one disgruntled eighteen-year-old to spread alarm and despondency through an entire neighbourhood, as we and some of our friends in SW12 learned to our cost when I delivered a tirade in French against our Spanish au pair girl's Swiss friend for throwing herself out of her job after a week, then living rough on Waterloo Station for a few nights, before landing on us without so much as a by-your-leave. Within a couple of weeks, both of them had disappeared into the night, taking half the local au pair population with them.

My advice, for what it's worth, is that it pays to buy British. It isn't just because they don't give you a blank, bolshy stare every time you so much as dare to open your mouth to them; or just because they're *au fait* with bread and butter pudding and occasionally laugh at one's jokes and don't come down every morning grousing about the weather. The joy of an English girl is that you know, however far her family may live from London and however often she feels homesick and has to ring them up, your telephone bill can never look as bad as it does with a foreign au pair beneath your roof.

Television

I hate to bang on about a thing, but for the middle-aged man, one of the greatest drawbacks to dinner parties is that, having knocked back a fair amount of pre-dinner drinks, troughed a larger than usual quantity of rich food, washed down with at least half a bottle of Côte du Rhone, and at the same time engaged in two hours' worth or more of small talk, often with total strangers, he is then expected (after yet more booze and heavy-handed quipping with the boys) to stagger through into the drawing room and keep going in similar vein for at least another hour before being released into the blessed cool and silence of the night air. No respite is afforded, no rest permitted. Close your eyes for a second and you are accused of being anti-social. Stop talking for a moment and you are a bore.

I've said it before and I'll say it again. At every dinner party at least half an hour should be set aside immediately after leaving the table in order that anyone who so wishes may be allowed to sleep. A ceasefire should be called on all serious conversation, and a general recharging of batteries all round not only permitted but demanded.

I have often thought seriously about introducing the post-prandial siesta at my own soirées. I feel sure it could quickly catch on and become as much a part of accepted social etiquette as embossed invitation cards and the Loyal Toast. The only serious danger is that there are some guests who might really get their heads down and be out for the rest of the proceedings. Me included. (See Plays, The Tendency of the Middle Aged to Nod Off in the First Acts of.)

Is it any wonder that the older one gets, the keener one is to spend one's evenings at home in front of the box? Not only is one not called upon to make conversation with it, but after a couple of drinks and a good meal, there is scarcely a programme on any channel (except possibly *Minder*) that is not guaranteed to have one (by one, I mean me) zizzing happily until dog-walking time. The arrival of Channel Four has merely added to the already wide choice of programmes I can sleep through.

Having discovered that I was missing almost every programme

I ever sat down to and was therefore even more badly equipped with small talk material at dinner parties, and in a desperate bid to revitalise my sex life (see Sex, the Middle-Aged Man and), I rented a video tape recorder so that I could be sure (a) of being in bed and reasonably lively at around the same time as my wife and (b) of being able to watch all those wonderful series and major documentaries that are the staple diet of modern conversation, when I was feeling altogether perkier.

Unfortunately, I now find that I sleep through most of the recordings too, whatever time of the day I play them, and have to start all over again at a later date. Not only does this mean that I have to keep buying more and more new tapes because every inch of the existing ones is taken up by unwatched programmes, but I am now so far behind in my viewing that by the time I finally get round to the highly acclaimed John le Carré series or the controversial documentary on the Shroud of Turin, they're repeating it anyway and I could have spared myself the expense.

I feel I ought to see someone about all this but can't decide whether it should be the Head of Programmes or a good doctor.

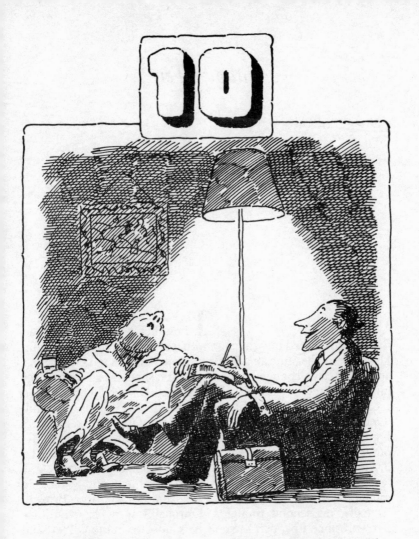

In which I reveal a typically middle-aged
inability to come to terms with inflation and
the cost of living, and offer some first hand
advice on how to survive an evening with a
life insurance salesman.

Chapter Ten

The other day, at a concert in Suffolk, I bumped into the man who was my first Creative Group Head when I became an advertising copywriter in 1964. He didn't appear to have changed a lot since I'd last set eyes on him over nineteen years previously. I obviously had, though, because when I called out 'John!' to him just outside the Gents, he said, 'Geoffrey!' But then I've noticed that a lot of middle-aged people I speak to have problems with names, especially mine. I, on the other hand, can always remember people from my past. I'll be driving along Oxford Street in a taxi and suddenly a face will come leaping out at me from a crowded pavement and without a moment's hesitation I'll say, 'Hudson!' or 'Jardine-Brown!' Actually, on second thoughts, I probably won't say 'Jardine-Brown!' since I happen to know he's a doctor in the Gilbert and Ellice Islands. There you are, you see, it's not only names and faces that I remember, but details of their private and professional lives that even they themselves have long since forgotten. In fact, so blessed am I with phenomenal powers of total recall that I have often tried to think up ways of harnessing my talent to some useful and lucrative purpose, such as a newspaper column or a television series. Leslie Welsh, after all, was a very big name in his day and I've no doubt they have been hunting for a suitable successor ever since.

Anyway, all that's by the by. The point is, not only did I immediately recognise John, but at the very sight of that domed head and that familiar lumbering walk, all sorts of incidents and conversations came flooding back into the forefront of my memory – like the occasion during the client meeting when the brand manager started outlining his company's thinking for the next year's television advertising and John, who had been scribbling furiously on the back of an envelope under the table, suddenly produced the piece of paper, as if from out of his pocket, with the words, 'How very interesting you should say that; we've been thinking along precisely the same lines ourselves.'

But perhaps the remark that sticks out most prominently in my mind is the one he made to me the day I broke the £1,000 a year barrier.

'You'll find the real difference comes,' he said, 'when you start earning fifteen hundred. I remember my wife and I felt we'd really made it because at last we could afford to buy Danish unsalted butter.'

Even now, all these polyunsaturated years later, I can still just remember what he meant. But, of course, when the great day finally arrived that my talents were properly recognised and my salary leapt to a princely £1,750, it didn't actually seem to make that much difference after all. Dinner for two at The Ark in Notting Hill Gate may only have come to £2.10.0d., with wine and service, a rented flat off Baker Street cost £3 a week, and £2 worth of 4-star would get you to Scotland and back in a Mini-Moke, but somehow, however much one earned, even in those days when inflation was something you did to your car tyres, it all seemed to disappear.

Being young and foolish, one supposed that the time would inevitably come when one was bound to earn more than one could spend. Somewhere around the £3,500 mark probably. And when that happened, one would be in a position to consider putting down the deposit on a little house in Fulham, investing a few bob a month in one of these unit trust schemes that smooth young men were always ringing up about; even getting married.

If only we had known then what we know now as we stagger into middle age on our pitiful £15,000 a year salaries, our crippling mortgages, our £20 a head restaurant bills plus VAT, and our family estate cars that swallow £2 of petrol between the garage and the front gate.

Could life really have been so simple in those days and were we so naïve that we could not see that the day when we would have a little bit left over was never going to come? And that property had to be the only worthwhile investment and that the only way to get on in this world is to buy first and worry about how you're going to pay for it afterwards?

Well, at least my caution paid off in one respect: I didn't marry young, devote my best years to raising a family and arrive at the age of forty only to spend my middle age making up for my lost youth. But at the same time I only just managed to scramble on to the property merry-go-round by the seat of my pants.

Today I'm a happily married man, content in the knowledge that my annual insurance premium bill is well over what my old friend John considered to be the salary of a man who had made it, and that at last there is actually a tiny amount left over at the end of the year. Just enough in fact to enable me to write out a cheque for the personal pension plan that the insurance man so persuasively sold me, and as a result to get the full tax relief.

God forbid . . .

In his book *Without Feathers*, Woody Allen describes how, over-come with self-loathing, he contemplates suicide by inhaling next to an insurance salesman. Actually, I'm not sure he'd need to go to quite such lengths. Just sniffing a proposal form would probably do the trick.

Insurance salesmen, who appear to occupy slightly more of one's time in middle age than one's own wife, are of course nothing more than highly trained extortionists. They have two methods of ensuring that you reach for your cheque book: fear and boredom. First of all they terrify you into realising that tomorrow morning, possibly earlier, various unforeseen tragedies are going to strike you and your family in quick succession. First, your house is going to burn down, bringing down the house next door with it and incidentally setting fire to a couple of adjoining fields of valuable barley, the smoke from which blinds a passing motorist in a brand new Rolls Royce Corniche who veers off the road into a tree, bringing a large branch down on the head of a passing Rodent Officer, killing him instantly and orphaning his family of eight. Next, you're going to remember that the rare nineteenth-century Turkish prayer mat with which you vainly tried to beat out the flames was not insured on an all-risks basis, even though you had been planning to call by the office that morning and do something about it. Thirdly, you're going to choose that moment to realise that you have forgotten to renew the insurance on the car which is smouldering cheerfully in what remains of the garage. And fourthly, you're going to step out into the road to wave down the fire engine only to be struck by a United Dairies milk float coming the other way and, as they wheel you into casualty, you're going to remember that thing about joining that health insurance scheme which you have been meaning to do something about for the past six months . . .

Having convinced you that, even as he is speaking to you, fate is, in the words of P. G. Wodehouse, quietly slipping the lead into the boxing glove, the salesman then reaches into his briefcase, draws out a pencil and pad which he fills with all manner of figures that would have had Bertrand Russell wondering if he was really up to 'O' Level, at the same time speaking fluent gibberish sprinkled with constantly recurring words like 'reversionary bonus', 'accelerator' and 'conversion option'.

One feels certain that, if only one dared to stop him in mid-flow and ask him to remind one of the meaning of these key words one might be in a position to crack the code, but since he has already been through it all once, to admit at the age of forty-three that one still hadn't quite grasped it, would be not only to make one look like some sort of mental defective but, more importantly, it might encourage him to bamboozle one into parting with even more of one's spare cash.

And so one sits there, nodding sagely, as he outlines the main differences between Increasable and Renewable Term Assurance, Whole Life Assurance with Profits, Endowment with Profits over a twenty- and twenty-five-year term, and Minimum Cost Endowment over the same two terms, trying desperately to give the impression that one is not just absolutely with him but actually a step or two ahead.

Occasionally, just occasionally, a glimmer of light breaks through the dark clouds of incomprehension, and to one's astonishment one hears oneself exclaiming, 'Aha, so the sum payable on the Endowment Sum Insured of £8,100 with bonuses at the end of twenty-five years will be at least £20,000 only provided that the average annual compound bonus rate has not been *less* than 3.68%!'

Unfortunately, like the man on holiday in Finland with only a basic phrase book to help him along the way, it is one thing to succeed in making the passer-by understand that you wish to find a doctor for your in-growing toenail, but quite another to follow up with a supplementary question relating to the fact that you have lost your wife in the supermarket or to make head or tail of his incomprehensible suggestions in reply.

The recognised method of calling a halt to the gruesome sales pitch is by announcing that everything he has said is most interesting and perhaps if he would be kind enough to leave all the material with you, you will mull over the various options in the coming few days and call him early next week. This he will readily agree to do and within minutes he will be out of your house and, you may suppose if you are young and inexperienced, out of your hair. We of maturer years, however, know better; because we know that if you leave the door open so much as a fraction of an inch, he'll be back and through it a week later like a rat up a drain, and then you'd really better start putting your hand on your inner pocket. These are lean and hungry men, trained to go straight for the cheque book and to show no pity to those weak enough not to know how to say no, and mean it.

The middle-aged, self-employed man with a family is their main target. They have ways of sniffing out the one whose portfolio does not quite come up to their exigent standards and, once they have the victim in their sights, they are down on him like a hawk on a vole.

Some they will allow to offer themselves voluntarily via worrying advertisements. One of the large insurance groups used to run one which looked like a strip cartoon. It was divided into four sections. The first showed a young man saying he was far too young to worry about boring things like pension plans. The second showed the young man, ten years on, telling himself cheerfully that there was still plenty of time to be thinking about that pension plan. The third depicted him in middle age, looking slightly concerned and declaring that he really should do something about that pension plan. In the fourth he was an old man on the threshold of retirement saying sadly, 'How I wish I'd done something about my pension . . .'

Those short-sighted enough not to see the logic that is staring them in the face must be tackled at close quarters, shaken by the throat and made to see the folly of their inactivity. This approach can be made in the form of an unsolicited telephone call – 'Mr Matthew, you won't know me, I'm from . . .' Nowadays, however, the 'friends of friends' method is proving extremely popular especially with the older salesman who has gone into the business rather late in life after being made redundant after twenty years as

Branch Manager in a firm specialising in bathroom and lavatory equipment. Anyone, no matter how skilled he may be at spotting an insurance salesman at 250 paces, can be forgiven for falling for this one. It even happened to me only a year ago.

We hadn't exactly lived in each other's pockets at Oxford, but I certainly recognised the name straightaway when he telephoned. A vague picture of a house filled with would-be secretaries somewhere near Folly Bridge swam into view from somewhere fairly deep in the sludge of my memory bank, and when he said he happened to be passing my neck of the wood later that week and thought he might look me up for old times sake, I was pleased and rather flattered that I should have made such a strong impression on him that he still remembered me all these years later.

We passed a pleasant hour or two, drinking tea and whisky and chatting about old times and old friends, even though some of them were not exactly razor sharp in my mind's eye. I was most interested to hear that he had moved to East Anglia and that he had two boys who were doing well at prep school, and I was naturally sorry to learn that he had been made redundant, and relieved to know that he had gone into the insurance business. As for the book on English wines that he was on the point of completing, I assured him that I would do the very best I could to think of a publisher who might be interested.

I thought little more about it until three weeks later when I was surprised to learn that once again he would be passing my door and had a project which he thought might be of interest to me.

Hallo, I thought. A joint publishing venture perhaps? An interest in a vineyard near Bury St Edmunds? A free week, all expenses paid, touring the vineyards of the Beaujolais on a comparative tasting? I couldn't have looked forward to seeing my old friend more.

Even when I was pouring him a second whisky and he enquired casually, *à propos* nothing in particular, whether there was anything in the insurance line that he might be able to help me out over, the penny didn't drop.

'Are you quite sure . . . cheers . . . you're fully covered?'

I said with a light laugh, 'Oh, I think so, thanks.'

'Life insurance up to scratch, is it?' he said.

I said that I appreciated his interest, but that in fact I had made a deliberate decision not to load myself with life insurances at this stage but to go all out on one of these low cost endowment mortgage jobs . . .

Even as I uttered the words I could see the gleam in his eye, as the excitement of the chase suffused his features.

'I think,' he said quietly, 'that the time has come for me to deliver my little speech about life insurance.'

Why I didn't boot him out there and then I shall never know. Perhaps insurance salesmen go through a crash course in hypnotism before they are loosed onto the unsuspecting public. All I can tell you is that this busy man-of-the-world sat there on the sofa, polite and unmoving, while this so-called friend of his tortured him with visions of a brave little wife, or rather widow, who, when she was not struggling to keep up appearances in front of her friends, was out scrubbing doorsteps and trying to interest Sothebys in his collection of book matches.

Like Customs officials, insurance salesmen must be trained to recognise the tiniest glimmer of guilt and fear in the eyes, because no sooner had the full horror of my irresponsible behaviour struck home than out had come the inevitable pad and pencil.

'Now supposing that tomorrow you fell under a bus, which God forbid, but just supposing for the sake of argument you did . . .'

The doctor to whom I was sent for the medical was unusually complimentary.

'Well, I must say,' he said to me as I stood there in my underpants, stomach sucked in, feeling every minute of my age as I rabbited on about 'carrying rather more weight than usual', 'sedentary occupation', 'meaning to go on a diet', etc, 'You've certainly kept your figure.'

I laughed and told him that was the trouble.

'No, no,' he said, 'I mean it.'

Either he was on a kickback from the insurance company or else he'd just been giving a check-up to Cyril Smith.

I replied with a sheepish smile and hurriedly pulled on my shirt.

'So,' he said, running an eye over his notes, 'you've just become a father for the second time in two and a half years. I think in the circumstances that this is a cause for celebration.'

I still cannot make up my mind whether the whole thing was some sort of elaborate joke. If so, then the laugh was very much on the insurance company, since I came away feeling so perky that thoughts of death could not have been further from my mind. Still, I really *must* do something about it one of these days. At my age, one can't afford not to.

In which I offer a simple office survival
guide for executives over forty. Includes a
shocking in-depth interview with a big
cheese in a top London advertising agency.
Also advice on how to suffer the office party,
the business trip, the business meeting and
the boot, without losing your dignity.

Chapter Eleven

It seems only the other day that the theory: 'If a chap hasn't made it by the age of forty, he's never going to make it at all' was being bandied about in pubs, clubs, dinner parties, office corridors and wherever else it is that people who make such pronouncements habitually meet. Nowadays, it would appear that a more realistic figure would be about twenty-seven. The briefest glance through the Situations Vacant columns shows that they are full of such ominous provisos as: 'If you're in your late twenties or early thirties we'd like to hear from you', and: 'Only applicants between twenty-five and thirty-five need apply. Only the other day I learned that the world creative supremo of one of Britain's biggest advertising agencies is all of thirty-three. What's more, I distinctly remember him arriving as a callow trainee at an agency where I was doing sterling work on behalf of Kellogg's Ricicles back in the middle sixties. I don't remember him as being particularly great shakes, but then not even I in my creative prime was ever able to conjure up prize-winning copy out of free offers for Noddy Bouncy Balls on the back of cereal packets.

Indeed, it was for this reason as much as any other that I left the business a year or two later and have been unemployed ever since. I was just over thirty at the time – a young man trembling on the brink of life. Nowadays I daresay I'd be considered a pipe and slippers case.

But is this in fact true or am I the unwitting victim of false rumour? Is it just another middle-aged neurosis that convinces me that if the policemen are getting younger, the captains and the kings of the business world are little older than schoolboys? Supposing, just supposing, I had stayed on in the advertising world, would I really now be nothing more than a has-been who never was?

For an answer to these and other questions I rang a contemporary of mine from my last agency. I cannot really remember now exactly what we worked on. Some shoe campaign possibly, but possibly not. Certainly in those days, a dozen years ago, we were both still very much at lieutenant level. I'd bumped into him once or twice since – on the slopes of a Swiss ski resort, in the Crush Bar at Covent Garden where, as a Friend of the Opera House, he was entertaining a client, and at a couple of dinner parties given by mutual friends. I could see he was getting on pretty well in my absence. Even so, I was rather surprised when, having been finally punched through by his secretary and explained what I was after, he told me that he'd be delighted to fix a meeting, but not for another three weeks as he was rather tied up at the moment.

I laughed it off as a blatant attempt to impress me, until, that is, I saw his office. Although perhaps not as spacious as some I have been into in my time, it gave all the appearance of belonging to a man who had come on in the world in no uncertain terms – a corner room overlooking the square, leather button-back sofa, silver-framed prints, the odd carefully placed antique . . .

I suppose I should have guessed that by now he'd be one of the top six men who actually run the whole caboodle. Looking at his expensive suit, his real leather briefcase with combination locks, his poised and confident air, the elegant way in which he tossed his secretary a bunch of keys and asked her if she'd be very sweet and do something with his car, it was just outside the front door on a double yellow line . . . it made me wonder if perhaps I'd been a fool to throw it all up so soon. Had I stuck it out, I'd surely have been up at the top there with him by now.

'Actually,' he said, lying back against the dark brown leather and sipping at his coffee, 'there aren't any old copywriters these days. You'd have been well over the hill by now. To give you an idea, the oldest creative man we've hired recently is thirty-seven and he's already been managing director of his own company.'

'But all those young men I started out with . . . ?' I said. 'That band of gilded youth . . . that brilliant generation that helped to fire the white heat of technology . . . the very warp and weft of swinging London . . . you mean to say . . .?'

'Out,' he said. 'Finished.'

'But where? What . . .?'

'Freelancing, some of them. Running pubs. Writing restaurant columns. Who knows? All I can tell you is that in our day there were 30,000 people in London working in advertising. Now there are half that.'

I suggested that I might have gone across to the executive side.

'You might have made it to the top,' he said, his voice tinged with serious doubt. 'Three of the men who run this company are under fifty. Mind you, the other three are forty or less.'

It crossed my mind to enquire why it was that a business that aimed to catch the attention of so many middle-aged and elderly citizens should be staffed entirely by people who had no concep- tion of what it was to be a member of either of those age groups – or, for that matter, had ever known what it is like to travel on a bus, but I let it pass. Doubtless, in the view of advertising people, those over the age of forty just don't have the spending power. They're certainly right in my case.

I said, 'But just supposing I had turned out to be so brilliant and indispensable and good at office politics that I had managed to pass the age of forty without getting the chop and was still in there with a chance at forty-three . . . ?'

He said, 'Well, we almost certainly wouldn't be able to sit here chatting like this in a chummy sort of way, and I'm afraid I'd have to turn you down for lunch and squash and that sort of thing. Drinkies after work in the pub and so on. Socially we'd have to take care we didn't meet outside the office either. No more dinner parties and what not.'

I said coldly, 'In my day, the whole point about advertising was that there was none of the dreadful seniority business you get in big old firms. Everyone mucked in together. It was always Christian names all round. You make it sound like public school, except that at least at school you could meet up with a chap in the hols even if he was in a junior study to you.'

He said, 'It would be for the good of both of us. Just in case I had to give you the sack, you see. So embarrassing if our wives had become bosom pals.'

I laughed and said, 'But you wouldn't sack someone with a good lively mind like mine would you?'

His face hardened. 'Everyone's worried about unemployment

these days, but that still doesn't stop people of a certain age getting complacent. You never know. It is possible to remotivate someone over forty, but there are always exceptions. Besides, you might suddenly decide to use our friendship in a very unuseful way. Unuseful to the company and unuseful to both of us. When you get to my position, the masterly touch of objectivity is all-important. People after all have got to listen to you, and if you can't be tough when you need to be tough, it'll show a year later. It may be all an act, but one has to have an edge if one wants to stay at the top.'

I told him that at his salary I could probably handle it.

He said, 'The salary is not important. It's the fringe benefits that count at my level. But it's true you'd expect to earn about £25,000 a year, plus a car, plus expenses. On the other hand, would you be able to sleep at night, knowing that you were responsible for £100,000,000 worth of business? And, more importantly, have you actually got it in you to lead? Remember the older you get, the more important self-motivation becomes. Infectious enthusiasm is what makes a company successful and when you're at the top it's all got to come from you. There's no one else.'

Having spent the past twelve years training myself against all the odds to get the bum on to the chair, the fingers on to the typewriter keys and the mind on to the business in hand – viz: knocking out a thousand words a day and keeping the children in socks – I felt like saying that if anybody wanted to know about self-motivation, then I was their boy. But then I suppose when you're an unemployable has-been of forty-three, it isn't easy to be taken seriously these days.

As I stepped out into the mid-morning sunshine and headed for Hatchard's for a relaxing browse before lunch at Searcy's Wine Bar in Chelsea, I couldn't help reflecting how lucky I was to have been sufficiently unencumbered at the age of thirty with dependants, mortgages, school fees – what one copywriter I used to know always referred to sadly as 'caught on a green hook' – to have escaped regular employment when I did. To say that I would recommend any man who is approaching middle age and still retains a vestige of his sanity to get out before they throw you out (and let's face it, fifty-five is chucking-out time in a lot of big firms these days), smacks badly of smugness. Besides, in ninety-nine cases out of a hundred, it would be a sheer impossibility. At the same time I feel duty bound to report that there is nothing like a spot of self-employment, with all its uncertainties, its lack of pension and paid holidays and its quarterly struggle with the VAT return, to keep the mind young and flexible, if not the body. Apart from anything else, it gets you out of that quaintest of all British tribal rituals . . .

The Office Party

Like all tribal rites, its origins are buried deep in the mists of time. All that anthropologists and sociologists can say with any degree of certainty is that, for some arcane reason, every year, about a week or two before Christmas, thousands of office workers willingly and apparently cheerfully submit themselves to several hours of indignity and torture at the hands of their fellow workers, in the sure and certain knowledge that if at any point in the proceedings they put so much as a small toe wrong, they could place themselves, their families and their whole lives in jeopardy.

For what may appear to the untutored eye to be nothing more than a jolly good knees up and, with a bit of luck, a hand up, too, is often nothing more than a thinly disguised appraisal board, and one's behaviour during that period of gay abandon could well decide one's future with the company. Indeed, the *on dit* is that some companies deliberately put off their New Year salary review until after the office party.

It is at times like this that the middle-aged man, his natural inhibitions loosened and the memory of his wife's disapproving features clouded by a liberal intake of Carafino Bianco, is at greater risk than at any other time in his professional year. Many's the executive who has found himself lured into all manner of hanky-panky by an unscrupulous secretary and wished he'd gone home after one quick drink as he said he would.

More anxious-making still is being reminded the following morning of behaviour of which one has not the faintest recollection.

A middleweight executive in an advertising agency I once worked in left one office party on his knees and arrived at his desk at lunchtime the following day to be faced by a copy of a letter from a senior colleague to an important client he'd invited along to the party for a drink after a long meeting. In it he apologised for his colleague's appalling behaviour, details of which were outlined at some length and included biting the client sharply on the ankle as he was leaving.

The fellow lived for the next week in mortal dread of the inevitable telephone call summoning him on high, until he discovered the whole thing was a hoax, dreamed up by the junior members of the staff to pay him back for some high-handed act or other from which they were still smarting.

If you must make a complete idiot of yourself by having it off with the relief receptionist behind, or indeed inside, the filing cabinet, for goodness' sake wait until the big cheeses have tactfully withdrawn and you have made your number with whoever it is who holds your future in his or her hands – preferably while you are still capable of coherent thought.

There are no hard and fast rules about how this delicate manoeuvre should be executed: with the minimum of palaver and the maximum of impact is probably as good a rule of thumb as any.

The moment your quarry is obviously at a loose end (why is it that everything one writes in this context seems to be fraught with double entendre and innuendo?), present yourself to him in as casual a way as possible, remind him of your name and department, chuck in a couple of complimentary remarks about the friendliness and generosity of the company and leave it at that. You cannot, and should not, do more.

Any attempt at party chitchat must be considered ill-advised in situations of this kind. Ditto name-dropping and attempts to place yourself socially.

A friend of mine, finding himself face to face with the chairman at an office party and momentarily at a loss for words, panicked, and for reasons that to this day he still cannot fully explain, heard himself saying, 'I understand you know Rear-Admiral Sandy Woodward?'

'Yes,' said the chairman. 'Why? Do you?'

'No,' he replied lamely, 'I'm afraid I don't myself.'

There is only one sure way to get through these gruesome events with any vestige of dignity and that is by making a firm dinner date with someone first. Anyone. Just so long as it isn't the relief receptionist.

The Business Trip

Happily, I gave up being employed before I became important enough to have to make long aeroplane journeys to Australia or Hong Kong – or, for that matter, short ones to Manchester and Glasgow. I have never known what it is like to find myself alone in a hotel restaurant in Frankfurt or Adelaide working my way through a steak dinner, at the same time trying to counter the waiters' pitying looks with an expression that is meant to imply that I needn't be alone, I just prefer it that way. Or, indeed, lying alone in a hotel room, staring blindly at some programme in a language I don't understand while I fight the temptation to call up the front desk and enquire where the action is in this town.

Those experienced in business travel assure me that at my age all I'd be up to after a day of meetings would be a quiet meal followed by an early night – unless, of course, I happened to work for a firm that did a lot of business in Tokyo, in which case it would be a noisy meal followed by a late night whether I felt like it or not.

I'm also assured that the only way to survive the long-distance flight is by ignoring all those tempting drinks and eats and in-flight movies starring Burt Reynolds, taking a couple of Mogadon, wrapping yourself firmly in a blanket and complimentary sleeping mask and missing the whole thing altogether.

Unfortunately, being temperamentally incapable of refusing a freebie, I sit there cheerfully accepting anything and everything that comes my way, from the flight plan to the complimentary cashews, and as a result, spend the first two days in my destination trying to give the impression of being a sophisticated man of the world with a brain that appears to have assumed the size and substance of a pickled walnut.

Merely another reminder that I was right to escape from the world of big business when I did.

The Business Meeting

In the days when I was a fresh-faced ad man, eccentric behaviour was tolerated and even expected from members of the creative department. Bored brand managers from Watford and Solihull did not come all the way to the West End of London to be bored even further by earnest people no different from the ones they spent every day with back at head office. They came for glamour, for laughs, for showbusiness; and the more talented a creative man was at dreaming up comic diversions to break the monotony of a long marketing presentation, the more likely the agency was to keep the account and the creative man his job.

One creative group head I worked with would not only arrive equipped with an array of stage props which he would whip out at carefully prearranged moments (his false nose and glasses always went down particularly well with the Ford client, I seem to remember), but he would suddenly interrupt a detailed analysis of sales figures in the north-east with the news that he had suddenly remembered an extremely important phone call he had to make. The entire meeting would come to a halt and a hush would descend over the assembled executives as he picked up the telephone and dialled a number.

'Won't keep you a moment longer than necessary,' he would say in a low, conspiratorial voice and then, 'Harry? Is that you? Oh, Roger here. I wonder if you'd be very kind and do me ten pounds each way, Lester Piggott in the three thirty?'

But of course everyone and everything has become much more serious since those days, and such frivolity is now firmly discouraged, or not even considered. Even in my day, and that was twelve years ago now, the man who, in the middle of a client meeting, suddenly turned to the chairman and asked if he could be excused as he had an urgent golf lesson, was not looked upon with favour. Though charm itself at the time, the chairman called him into his office the following morning and enquired politely if his lesson had been a success.

'Yes, thank you, sir,' replied the hapless executive.

'Excellent, excellent,' said the chairman. 'Well you'll certainly have plenty of time to put it all into practice from now on. Goodbye.'

The Boot

There's nothing funny about getting the sack. Certainly not these days and certainly not after the age of forty. It is shocking, humiliating, infuriating and depressing, though not necessarily in that order.

In my parents' day, being fired was only slightly less shaming than being caught in bed with the vicar's wife. It was not a subject fit for discussion in polite society.

In these recessive times, however, when whole firms are being laid off at a stroke, redundancy, as it is now known, is nothing to be ashamed of. Not only do respectable men deliberately get themselves chucked out so they can collect the redundancy pay, but the boot can actually launch some people into wonderful new careers.

More often than not, however, the sack comes like a bolt from the blue and you're the last one to be told. The friend of mine who was told by his boss, 'We wouldn't want to lose the sound of your little piccolo in our big orchestra,' could easily be forgiven for believing the remark was meant as a compliment. He certainly took it as such until the people from Office Services came to take away his desk.

There are various recognised tactics which can be brought into play should the boot appear to be in the wind. If cunningly employed, they might help to fend off the catastrophe that is about to be visited upon you.

Ploy 1: On the principle that it is never easy to sack anyone with whom you enjoy a close personal relationship, get your wife to ring up the boss's wife and ask them both to dinner.

Ploy 2: Devise some brilliant new money-saving efficiency scheme for the firm.

Ploy 3: Carry the war into the enemy's camp. I know of one enraged executive who left a large carving knife on his boss's desk, covered in tomato ketchup. Attached to it was a label with the words, 'I found this in my back. I believe it belongs to you.'

In the event of the sack actually being given, all need not be lost. Try asking, 'May I come back after my operation?' Or simply do as a friend of mine did. Not knowing what the procedure was upon receiving the sack he returned, quiet and uncomplaining, to his office and carried on with his work as if nothing had happened. His colleagues knew nothing about it, so they said nothing. Accounts, not having received notification of his imminent departure, continued to pay him in the normal way. When it was finally discovered, some weeks later, that he was still there, his boss hadn't the heart to put him through it all over again. As far as I know, he's still at his desk.

I'm only glad I'm not.

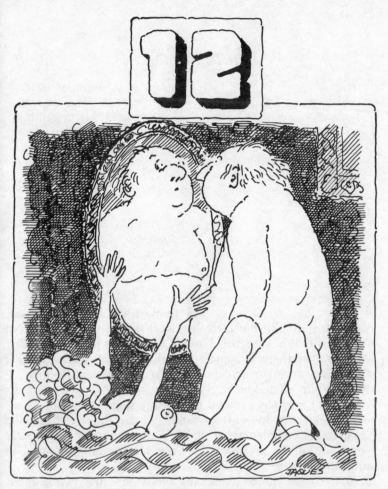

In which I tackle the thorny subject of sex
for those of advancing years – how to bring
one's marriage up to sexual scratch; how to
have an affair; how to cope with the younger
woman; how to increase your sex appeal –
with and without artificial aids; how to be a
middle-aged bachelor; how to get the best
out of your vasectomy.

Chapter Twelve

I think it was Beryl Bainbridge who came up with the idea that what distinguishes men from women is that a woman is blessed with a complete personality because everything is contained within a single package, as it were; whereas a man is made up of two quite separate elements – the chap himself and his winkle.

I cannot honestly pretend that at any stage in my life I have found myself at odds with my winkle, or that the wretched thing has ever got completely beside itself and gone rushing off after some sex object or other with me tearing along behind in unwilling pursuit.

At the same time, I am only too aware that of the many preoccupations with which men find themselves having to grapple between the ages of forty and sixty, none is more constantly in the forefront of their minds than sex. How's-your-father, hanky-panky, Ugandan discussions, Sportsnight with Coleman – call it what you will, thoughts of it are said to wander into the average male brain approximately once every seven minutes. For all the good it does most of us.

Those who have enjoyed a busy and varied sex life in their youth are keen to prove to themselves, and others, that, despite general physical deterioration all round, there's one corner of the system that continues to function as well as, if not better than, it ever did. Those for whom sex has never quite come up to the very high scratch they have always been led to believe it should, are concerned to put things in order and, if possible, to make up for lost time before it is too late. As for those sexual lunatics who will go to any lengths and run any risk for the sake of a spot of legover, the older they get, the more undiginified and shameless their pursuit of pleasure.

All too often in middle age, everything seems to be conspiring to transform sex from a jolly, carefree activity to be indulged in whenever and wherever possible into a gloomy obsession on a level somewhere between a dentist appointment and a visit from the VAT inspector.

Some married men can truthfully claim to enjoy a permanently warm, fruitful, loving relationship with their wives, unclouded by boredom, jealousy or a long series of unresolved minor differences that together add up to an insurmountable barrier. Not many, however. Most chunter on for years in a state of sexual and emotional indifference which they have learned to think of as contentment, until suddenly something occurs to bring them face to face with each other, e.g. the children grow up and leave home, if not physically, then emotionally and sexually, and a couple's whole reason for remaining together disappears overnight. They start introducing attractive young boyfriends and girlfriends who, if they don't drive you insane with jealousy, merely remind you, as if you needed reminding, that you are not nearly as young as you thought you were.

Half-hearted attempts are made to resume conjugal relations, but the embers are far too cool to catch and, before he knows what, the middle-aged husband's fancies lightly turn to thoughts of nubility.

But can a twenty-year-old girl really be expected to get excited over a thinning cranium and thickening waist? The spectre of impotence begins to raise its ugly head (or rather, it doesn't). Alcohol proves not to be the great aphrodisiac it's cracked up to be – not after the third whisky and soda and eleven o'clock at night it doesn't, anyway.

And even if, like most, one is a stranger to the proverbial brewer's, then there's always premature ejaculation to worry about (for those with a history of quick, secretive, guilt-making wanking) or delayed ejaculation (for the ones who for some reason suddenly start mistrusting their wives) or embarrassingly long refractory periods between erections (for those who, if they did but know it, are almost certainly suffering from nothing more serious than age).

Other considerations apart, the very image of one's white, corpulent shape, striking attitudes in some strange bedroom at one o'clock in the morning is so deeply unappealing to contemplate as to cause one to retire before one has even been brought to the starting gate.

And yet, apart from one friend of mine who announced at the age of forty-one that he had retired from the game for good and that there was absolutely no question of a last-minute comeback, I know of no one over the age of forty who has shown the slightest signs of flagging or failing in his enthusiasm for the opposite sex – or in some cases for his own. And while I cannot pretend to be an acknowledged expert on the subject – in theory or in practice – I feel I should be failing those of my readers who have stuck with me up till now, through the gritty unrewarding world of false teeth, hair transplants, Bullworkers and life insurance, if I did not at this stage offer them a few words of comfort, cheer and, who knows, even useful advice, in this the most inspiring, yet testing, area of middle-aged life.

As a jolly lady sex therapist I know is forever reminding her patients, it's all in the mind and mostly inaccurate anyway. Sex, whatever you may have heard or read to the contrary, is not just for the young. It does and should go on well into old age, and the one sure way of enjoying it is by being as relaxed and free of fear and inhibitions as you possibly can. Having grasped this simple principle, how should one set about putting it into practice?

With the wife

In his excellent novel *A Married Man*, Piers Paul Read's principal character, a successful barrister, develops a complaint he calls Ilychitis. Named after a character in a short story by Tolstoy entitled *The Death of Ivan Ilych*, the symptoms of this essentially middle-aged disease are deep melancholy combined with a sense of enormous dissatisfaction with everything in his life – especially with his twelve-year-old marriage to Clare. So totally does Ilychitis seize mind and body that, except in the very rarest of circumstances, there is no known cure. Whatever the outcome, be it an affair with the wife of a friend or entry into a closed monastic order, it is more or less guaranteed to end in tears.

Given, however, that things have not reached quite so far beyond the point of no return and that one is reasonably serious about getting things going again in the connubial five-footer, here are one or two little hints that might help.

(a) Try closing the bedroom door for once. Parents with small children fall into the habit of sleeping with the door open so that eventually they take lack of privacy for granted. They think nothing of the fact that when the children grow older they lock their bedroom doors when they want to be left alone or the bathroom door when they are feeling modest, and yet they themselves attempt to carry on in the most intimate way knowing that at any moment anyone, be it the children, the au pair or the dog, could walk in on them without so much as a by-your-leave.

(b) Try sex on Sunday afternoon. The English have a curious habit of assuming that sex is only on for a few minutes last thing at night. Not that there is anything to be said against midnight frolics *per se*. However, when both of you are knackered after a busy day of board meetings or a ding-dong with the children or a heavy dinner party or possibly all three, a long, vigorous and mutually satisfying bout of Sportsnight with Coleman is unlikely to be seriously on the cards, however, much both parties feel it ought to be. Now, on a wet Sunday afternoon, on the other hand, with the children out for a long tea with friends and the heating switched up and inhibitions down . . .

(c) By and large, well-meaning books on how to achieve a warm and loving relationship are to be avoided by the middle-aged in favour of common sense and spontaneity. I remember once reading a book called *The Sensuous Woman* which recommended all sorts of elaborate ways for a woman to bring her husband up to scratch. They ranged from such doubtful delights as The Butterfly Flick, the Silken Swirl, the Hoover and the Whipped Cream Wiggle, to surprising him by having the bedroom completely done over with mirrors and fake leopard skin. While in principle I would, were I a bored forty-five-year-old brand manager, approve of the idea of my wife rowing herself unexpectedly into my office one lunchtime bearing a delicious picnic, knowing my luck, just as we were beginning to get the hang of nibbling on each other between nibbles of caviare and pungent cheeses, the lady from Accounts would walk in.

With other women

Rarely can affairs involving married couples be carried on without someone getting badly hurt. Alastair Trumpington in Evelyn Waugh's *Put Out More Flags* managed it:

'Since marriage he had been unfaithful to Sonia for a week every year, during Bratts Club golf tournament at Le Touquet, usually with the wife of a fellow member. He did this without any scruple because he believed Bratts week to be in some way excluded from the normal life of loyalties and obligations: a Saturnalia when the laws did not run. At all other times he was a devoted husband.'

However, while there is certainly something to be said in favour of what the eye doesn't see, or the ear hear etc, few middle-aged men are as lacking in conscience as Alastair Trumpington. Or indeed blessed with such perfect opportunities and compliant partners.

On the whole, affairs are extremely hard work, involving as much mental as physical agility as the man desperately tries to ensure that the latest story he spins his wife will stand up to the closest scrutiny and that he gets to the love nest, gets on with it and gets back again at the time he said he would. Obviously this is marginally easier for a man who works in an office than it is for a man who operates from his own home. 'Sorry, darling, another of these wretched late meetings,' is virtually unchallengable, especially down a telephone, whereas the man who suddenly starts taking the dog out for three or four hours on end in the early evenings has got a bit of explaining to do.

But then, of course, there is the world of difference between the brief encounter on the business trip/golfing holiday and what is loosely known as 'having an affair'. This, too, can be sub-divided into three categories:

(a) The thing – as in 'He's having a bit of a thing with his secretary.'

(b) The arrangement, whereby a couple set up an extramarital establishment in a basement flat in Kentish Town. (The kept mistress is rather a thing of the past and only for those who by some lucky chance are unencumbered by mortgages, school fees etc.)

(c) The extramarital romance, which is basically the same as (b) but implies a tinge more seriousness and hopes for a degree of sympathy.

No matter in which category the discontented husband lands himself, he can be sure of one thing: no matter how plausible his excuses and how cunning his deceit, his wife will know he's up to no good, and sooner or later he will know that she knows. And so heavily will the guilt of his infidelity hang upon him that one day, consciously or unconsciously, he will give himself away, and when that happens he will, possibly for the first time in his life, have to start making some real decisions. There's nothing like an affair for raising a chap's morale, but if it has to be paid for by some of the most wretched misery a wife can ever know, one might be advised to ask oneself if it is all really worth the candle.

But of course all this gloomy philosophising presupposes that the discontented fellow on the lookout for an affair can actually find someone to have it with.

The American journalist, William Attwood, writing on the subject recently, announced confidently, 'The middle years are, paradoxically, a period of burgeoning sexual opportunity for many men. This is when the once elusive and temperamental women we pursued in our youth now beckon like Lorelei – at forty or forty-five – along with certain younger ones who, perhaps for psychological reasons, prefer their men friends older.'

Lucky old him, that's what I say. But then, of course, middle-aged Americans tend to make even more of a meal over sex than we do, and one should always take everything they have to say on the subject with a pinch of salt, viz: 'I wouldn't bet ten bucks that any of my male friends has been consistently faithful, sexually, to his wife.'

At the same time, he warns, 'If you are tempted, married or not, to make the most of these midlife opportunities, then at the very least take care to observe three practical taboos: never with wives of friends, never with fellow employees, and never with women under twenty-five. These three categories are the ones most likely to create all kinds of trouble for the philandering male – indiscretion and emotional complications being the most common.'

I am not, I am happy to say, qualified to comment on categories one and two. However, I did once as a bachelor have a bit of a thing with a nineteen-year-old.

The Younger Woman

Until I met her, I would never have believed it possible that a man of my age, taste and experience could have had his head turned by a slip of a girl to such a degree that he would take to dressing up in jeans and T-shirts, sitting up until all hours with kids who would have been too young for him when *he* was young, smoking exotic cheroots, listening to obscure pop groups and discussing the meaning of life, prancing about in louche discotheques and attempting to force himself into sexual positions that were, in the words of a friend of mine's nanny, 'Not funny and not clever'.

In my mad, geriatric passion, I would try to kid myself that I was her destiny, knowing all the time that there were many other men of all ages and all persuasions in her life and in her bed. Never before or since have I known such jealousy. By comparison, Othello's was merely a moment of mild irritation.

One evening she gave a party to which I was invited, along presumably with any other man who happened to fancy his chances. Intending to numb my sensibilities slightly and ensure that I arrived with every appearance of indifference, which I felt sure would be bound to arouse her interest, I consumed an entire bottle of Liebfraumilch in my flat first, went for a little lie down and woke at five the following morning feeling like death with the morning tea. As allergy treatment of a peculiarly drastic kind I cannot recommend it highly enough.

One is always hearing about older men making fools of themselves with girls half their age. All I can say is that if that is any indication of how a normally sensible, level-headed fellow can carry on in his thirties, I dread to think how far an over-excitable fifty-five-year-old could go off the rails if he put his mind to it.

The ill-informed would doubtless dismiss such antics as the typical behaviour of a silly old fool.

We who are better informed know that it is nobody's fault. It's all to do with pheromones about which I would like to say a word or two. These are undetectable natural scents which act on the olfactory organs and affect the way we react to others socially and sexually. The one that attracts women to men is called androstenone. We all possess the stuff to a greater or lesser extent. However, should we feel that, for some reason best known to Himself, the Almighty has decided to sell us short, we can always top up with a few squirts of the mysteriously named Aeolus 7.

Quite how the manufacturers in Long Ditton have managed to

capture something as primordial and undetectable as sex appeal and actually get it into an aerosol can is beyond me. It has been suggested by one wag that they must boil down Sean Connery's underpants.

The idea is to spray it on to some part of your clothing that gets waved around a lot, such as your cuffs, march into a room full of people and, lo and behold, before you know what, you're surrounded by beautiful women wishing to make inordinate demands on your astonished body.

'Get to first base every time with Aeolus 7,' declares the advertising, and by way of proving the point, various flattering comments from magazines and newspapers are quoted, ranging from sublime: 'This stuff makes Petunia want to screw like a bunny' – *Oui Magazine*, to the plain dotty: 'Minute quantities were sprayed on a chair in a dentist's waiting room. Women patients made straight for the chair' – *Sunday Times*. Proof, if proof were needed that some women are so desperate that they'll throw themselves at anything.

Various scientific tests have been carried out, but although, as the manufacturers point out, other factors such as confidence, experience, age, time of the day, etc. are bound to play a part in making up a woman's mind as to whether or not she fancies a man, 'the number of persons requesting refunds is minuscule in relation to total sales'.

Now, I don't think I'm being unnecessarily immodest when I say that this is not the sort of product that would interest me in the normal course of events. I may not be the talk of the Ladies' Powder Room, but I think I am perfectly capable of persuading a young lady to join me for a show and supper afterwards without having to call upon the services of an aerosol can. In the interests of pure research, however, I decided to carry out a small, controlled experiment of my own.

I began by trying it out on my wife. Unfortunately, in my efforts to aim the spray at exactly the right spot on the sleeve of my faithful old black pullover, I misfired slightly and hit the typewriter. (Any hopes I might have been harbouring that, on the principle of the dentist's chair, she would suddenly demonstrate an overwhelming desire to type out my manuscript, have so far proved to be unfounded.)

I went downstairs for lunch, taking care to give the dog a wide berth. This stuff is supposed to affect animals in the most unexpected ways, and to be suddenly mounted by a Kerry Blue

Terrier while pouring oneself a dry sherry can't be a lot of fun for anyone – least of all the dog.

Was it my imagination, or did I catch my wife out of the corner of my eye looking at me rather more intently than is her wont? I said nothing. Neither, I am afraid, did she.

Even when the cheese and biscuits had been and gone and we'd stood shoulder to shoulder at the sink and still nothing untoward had passed between us, I decided the time had come for a little gentle prompting.

'Have you noticed anything different about me today?' I said at last.

'No,' she said.

'All right, then,' I said, 'put it another way. You've been looking at me in rather an odd way for the last half an hour. Why?'

'It's that pullover,' she said.

'Yes?' I said. 'Yes?'

'It's gone through at the elbows, it doesn't fit you any more, and if you don't chuck it out, I will.'

A day or two later, I revealed all. She read through the literature, an expression of deep disbelief troubling her features that things had come to such a pretty pass that her husband had felt obliged to sink to this. Finally, she looked up.

'Well, funnily enough,' she said, 'it did strike me as rather odd that you had suddenly taken to putting your arms round me and talking in that silly, put-on voice.'

Phase Two of my experiment took place in a pub in Chelsea. A reporter from the *Sunday People* claimed that in similar circumstances, his pheromoned tie 'seemed to clear a way through the crowded bar,' and that within seconds of ordering a drink, 'a blonde was at my side asking my name'.

The girl who came up to me had dark hair, but her approach was no less blunt and to the point.

'Excuse me,' she said, 'but is that your Citroen CX parked outside?'

I said that it was.

She said, 'I thought so. I wonder if you'd mind moving it? I can't get out.'

Phase Three resulted in an unfortunate episode involving my milkman and a Doberman Pinscher which does not bear retelling at this point in the proceedings.

They say that, of course, other factors can contribute to the success or otherwise of this product.

The most obvious, of course, is the way in which one makes one's initial approach. One is after all a little out of practice at the age of forty plus, and it's all too easy to botch things before they have even got under way. Try, for example, smoothing your way up to a fashionably scruffy twenty-year-old in the Chelsea Potter in the King's Road in your hand-pressed Calvin Kleins, your £20 Ricci Burns hairdo and your Paco Rabanne for Men, and your suggestive small talk could well be greeted by expressions of amused disbelief.

At the same time, there are few young girls who are not impressed by a long, low bonnet, a nice fat wallet and the promise of far horizons. Unfortunately, however, there are occasions when even the grandest gestures are not enough, as a friend of mine discovered when, in a moment of spontaneous enthusiasm he suggested to a beautiful young girl he had just met at a party that they should hop into his speedy roadster, nip down to Heathrow and catch whichever happened to be the next flight out, wherever it happened to be bound – Rome, Sydney, San Francisco, Hong Kong. It was his bad luck and miserable timing that there was only one more flight out that night and it was going to Manchester.

Generally speaking, one is better off making one's pass in the less exuberant and less expensive surroundings of a restaurant, which is where the majority of potential affairs appear to blossom – or not, depending on how you go about these things. And for those of middle age who have either forgotten what approach works and what doesn't, or perhaps never really knew in the first place, I offer this basic, though by no means comprehensive, guide:

Whatever they may try to kid you otherwise, women nearly always respond to the straightforward, sexual approach. A happily married magazine editor I know in her late thirties was understandably taken aback, not to say mildly irritated, when a forty-four-year-old advertising manager she had invited out to lunch with a view to drumming up some business, immediately launched into a long spiel about his sex drive and how fit and sporting he was and how much keener he was on sex now than twenty years ago and how much better at it and how happily married he was and what beautiful children he had and what a great relationship he and his wife enjoyed in bed but how sometimes he wondered if she was up to satisfying his huge appetite and was she ever free for dinner, he often worked late in the office and didn't she agree that the most important thing in life was living it to the full and knowing how to work hard and play hard . . .?

Yes, she replied, when finally he drew breath long enough to take a swig of Sancerre, she couldn't agree more. However, when one is six months pregnant, all that sort of thing becomes largely academic. Collapse of sexy party.

She didn't blame him for trying, or indeed for the transparency of his approach. In different circumstances, she admits, she might well have fallen for it. She was only disappointed that he should so badly have misread the enthusiasm of her invitation and her generally friendly interest in him.

As she said later, 'At least for once I was spared the old my-wife-doesn't-understand-me ploy. That sort of thing might still work with much younger women, but at my age the last thing I'd want to take on would be somebody else's mess.'

Equally guaranteed to fail as an approach is, 'What I'm really looking for is a new mother for the children.' This may be heart-breakingly true, but for the mature woman with her eye to a spot of real passion and romance, all this means is either 'I need a cheap babysitter', or 'I am recently divorced and what the hell am I going to do with the six children on the weekends I get access?'

Other total turn-offs I have to report from my extensive researches are:

* Making it quite clear you assume she's coming home with you after dinner.
* Heavy after-shave.
* Short socks that reveal white hairy legs when you sit down.
* Arriving for dinner at her place and announcing, as she draws the roast beef from the oven, that you are not only vegetarian but a wholefood fanatic to boot.
* Dandruff.
* Letting yourself be caught looking into the nearest mirror.
* Halitosis.
* Letting yourself be caught treating yourself to a quick burst of mouth spray.
* The frequent interpolation of unnecessary and incomprehensible foreign words and phrases.
* Constant reference to all the first nights, private views, parties and other social events you have recently attended. In short, the unspoken challenge to a woman to try to top this is unlikely to be

taken up with very much enthusiasm. Ditto blatant intellectual and cultural sizing up. A young woman I know was once asked out to dinner by a middle-aged man for the first time and within seconds of sitting down at the table he said, 'Now then, how well up are you on your Shakespeare Sonnets?' She was not impressed.
* Ferociously hairy chests and gold bullion that give women the impression that, as one friend described it, '*Everything's* coming at you.'
* Nylon sheets.

Of the ploys that, although not foolproof, are far more likely to pave your way to success, the following are well-tried favourites:

* Making her feel comfortable and secure by getting her to talk about herself, not rushing things, and not allowing your disappointment to show when she says no.
* If you're being entertained at her place, offering to wash up/clear the table/make the coffee etc. In short, make it clear that you are a thoughtful, caring human being who is not there just for the food and the action. (At the same time, resist the temptation to suggest fixing the bookshelves/plumbing the sink/taking the dog for a walk. You don't want to start looking and sounding like a husband before you've become a lover.)
* Avoiding all talk of unhappy marriages, broken love affairs, analysts, mental anguish, the meaning of life etc. On the other hand, I am assured on the very best authority that the twisted intellectual approach can often work a treat – e.g. 'I'm having terrible trouble with my latest novel and I think you're just the person who can help me.' Of course, it helps if you happen to write novels. Actually, being an orthopaedic surgeon or a criminal lawyer will probably serve you just as well. Women are invariably interested in people who are passionately interested in what they do. If you happen to be an enthusiastic traveller in ball bearings that may be another matter altogether (see Mid-stream, the Middle-Aged Man's Attitude towards Changing Jobs in).
* If you feel the need to base your style on anyone, base it on Michael Caine. According to a recent survey, he is the film star mature women fancy more than any other. More even than Reynolds, Redford or Eastwood. It's the combination of humour, good manners and vulnerability that gets them. So, if up to now you've been thinking Burt or Bob or Clint when you take a lady

out (or in), don't. Think Michael. Even Burt and Bob and Clint are beginning to these days.

* The approach that I long to try but so far have never dared is the one used to devastating effect by an old army buddy of Art Buchwald's. The story goes something like this:

So intrigued was Art by this apparently unprepossessing fellow's high scoring rate with women that finally he could contain his curiosity no longer and announced that he would be accompanying him on his next outing.

They had a few drinks, met up with some girls and went back with them to their place. They had a few more drinks and things were starting to get moving when Art heard his buddy telling his girl that he really didn't think there was a lot of point in carrying on any further along those lines. When she asked why, he was unwilling to divulge details but finally, after much coaxing on her part, he revealed that he was impertinent . . . no, that wasn't the right word . . . important . . . no . . .

'You don't mean to say,' she said, 'that you're impotent?'

'Impotent,' said the soldier. 'That's the word.'

'Oh, you poor man,' said the girl. 'Isn't there anything . . .?'

'Nothing,' he said. 'I'm sorry.'

'Oh, I'm sure you're wrong,' she said. 'I have an idea or two that I think might help.' And taking him gently by the hand, she led him off in the direction of the bedroom.

'I doubt it,' he said glumly. 'you're welcome to try but I think you're wasting your time.' On which note the door was closed firmly behind them.

They returned half an hour or so later looking extremely pleased with themselves.

'There your are,' said the girl. 'What did I tell you?'

'Well,' said the soldier grinning modestly, 'I must admit you were right. I'd never have believed it possible.'

Now then, before you kick yourself at never having thought of that one before, and rush off to give it a whirl, remember: you can only fool some of the girls some of the time, as Buchwald discovered when he turned to his partner and said: 'Hey, that sounded good. Why don't you and me try a little of the same?'

'You filthy beast,' she replied. 'Get your hands off me. What sort of a girl do you think I am?'

The Bachelor

Most of what I have had to say up till now could as well apply to the middle-aged bachelor as to the married man – if such a creature can still be said to exist nowadays. (The bachelor, I mean.) I am constantly hearing stories via my wife of divorced women in their mid to late thirties grousing about the dearth of eligible single men over the age of forty. As one who was a bachelor himself until quite recently, I resent the implication that chaps who are not married by a certain age are necessarily queer, crashing bores, or in some way unsuitable lover material.

Take my friend Charles, for example. I do not believe anyone could seriously accuse him of being a sexual washout. A bit of an old romantic perhaps. A little on the sentimental side maybe. Rather square even. And why not? Old-fashioned men of principle are all too thin on the ground these days, to my way of thinking, and this country is all the poorer for it (see Heath, Edward).

As Charles himself put it to me once in his usual forthright manner, 'What people seem to forget is that some of us were brought up in the good old days before the so-called Permissive Society reared its ugly head – when men were men and women were women, and everyone knew where they stood.

'I mean, I can remember a time, it seems only yesterday, when *Men Only* meant humorous articles by Patrick Campbell, and the nearest thing you could get to a girlie magazine was *Health and Efficiency*. And since all the women in it appeared to have undergone plastic surgery, none of us had the faintest clue what the form was anyway. Except Gerry Harrison. But then, of course, he had a French mother, so he didn't count.

'The point is, when I was a young man, women didn't go in for all this casual, take-it-or-leave-it horizontal jogging that seems to lie at the very root of our society today. At least the women I met didn't.

'Whatever happened to good, old-fashioned, innocent romance? That's what I'd like to know. My theory is that all that sort of thing went out with private dances. Ah, those were the days. Big striped tent, poles wrapped in coloured bog roll, cold chicken and ham dished out by elderly biddies in black, bread rolls flashing past your ears like tracer, Chappie d'Amato and his Orchestra, bulky birds with chests you could park a Land Rover on, shoulders like stevedores, the Last Waltz, lights out, tongue like half a lemon sole exploring your back teeth. Now that's what I call romance.

'Shall I tell you the last time I danced? I mean, shall I tell you the last time I actually gathered a pretty young thing in my arms and stepped it lively across the French chalk? I can't remember. That's how long it was.

'Goodness knows how young people meet each other these days. Mincing about in leotards in some disused school gymnasium in Kentish Town, no doubt, at one of these so-called encounter sessions or some such namby-pamby, self-congratulatory get-together, dreamed up by a load of homo, left-wing, bloody do-gooders who are too puny and inhibited and ugly to put on a suit and tie and stand in a roomful of decent people with a glass of whisky and soda in one hand and half a dozen assorted nuts in the other, and carry on proper, useful conversation about the price of long-term gilts like any other self-respecting civilised Englishman.

'But then in those days, of course, we believed in calling a spade a spade. Or a wog, to be precise. And we were none the worse for that, say I. People knew their place in those days, particularly women. It's a pity one can't say the same thing about them today.'

Now, how in the world women can say there are no eligible single men around when there are people like Charles going begging, beats me.

Birth Control

Sorry to bring you back to earth with a bump (or not, if you're careful), but just in case any middle-aged reader should be labouring under the odd misapprehension re this thorny subject, a cautionary word might not be altogether out of order. Impregnation does not, whatever anyone may have led you to believe otherwise, equal virility. Bankruptcy possibly, paternity almost certainly, but frankly, there's nothing funny or clever about becoming a father at fifty without really meaning to (see Chapter 7). It is also unwise to assume that after a certain age (a) the chances of getting someone pregnant are pretty remote, (b) women can be relied upon to take care of that side of things, and (c) if anything goes wrong, you will be in a position to fulfil that cheerful promise that you will always take care of her.

Given that withdrawal, which has always worked before, suddenly doesn't, and that there are those for whom the whole operation is touch and go enough as it is without the added complication of condoms, the answer could well be . . .

Vasectomy

This was discovered by Michael Parkinson in the early seventies, never a man to allow minor surgery to put him off his stroke. Is it any wonder that thousands have followed his example by flocking to birth control centres up and down the country ever since?

Of course, in India, where they tried to introduce the idea some years ago, they gave a free transistor radio to every vasectomee. In this country they content themselves with giving applicants a hard time – or at least the women in charge do, if my friend Lorenzo's experiences are anything to go by.

Divorced from his wife and happily established with his live-in girlfriend, he came to the conclusion that middle-aged parenthood was not for him and rang the local birth control people. The phone was answered by a lady doctor who listened to what he had to say and replied that, before she could take the matter any further, he would have to come and see her for a counselling session. He pointed out that no amount of counselling was going to help at that stage since he had already made up his mind and that's all there was to it. He wasn't a child. She replied that she was very sorry, but if he wished to proceed further, she would have to ask him to come in, and bring his wife with him. He explained that he and his wife were divorced. In that case, she said, the woman whith whom he had a permanent liaison.

At this point, he decided enough was enough. This was a deliberate blow on behalf of the women's liberation movement and if it wasn't, how come they never made a fuss when women asked for help with family planning? He added that he had never considered himself the owner of his spouse's body and certainly saw no reason to change his point of view at this stage in his life. They were *his* goolies, and if he wanted to have them vasectomised, it was no concern of hers.

She replied that she was very sorry; she didn't make the rules. . .

In the end he had it done privately. And just as well, too, he decided. If he thought his run-in with the lady doctor was humiliating, it was as nothing compared with the experience of a friend of his who made the mistake of actually submitting to the demands of the local clinic harpies and arrived at 9.30 sharp for his operation to find only women in charge there too.

'Trousers off, out there,' one of them barked at him, and before he knew what, he was sitting in a freezing corridor at the end of a long row of equally trouserless and cowed men, who were summoned one by one, given an extremely painful local anaesthetic and, after a brief lie down, sent packing.

Lorenzo's operation cost him a bob or two, but at least he got a private room, a general anaesthetic and a night to get over it. On the other hand, he was expected to shave himself.

'I don't know if you're ever tried shaving your balls,' he said, 'but it's considerably more tricky than you might suppose. I mean, for a start there are all these knobbly bits one keeps nipping off. . .'

The operation itself couldn't be more straightforward. 'A quick slice down the side of the scrotum, a snip of whichever tube it is that puts the lead in the pencil, and that's it. You feel a bit sore for a couple of days afterwards, as if somebody had given you a sharp kick in the orchestras, so you don't feel like going in for anything strenuous, like a three-legged race at the school sports. And anyway, you've got these dissolvable stitches to think about. Unfortunately, mine dissolved before the wound healed, which was a bit of a blow as we were going on holiday, and I'm rather keen on my swimming. I thought about taping up my balls with surgical tape, but that seemed a little on the strong side, so in the end I settled for Sellotape. The only trouble is that after you've been in the sea for a bit, it tends to come away, so I had to spend most of my holiday on Sidmouth Beach struggling under a bathing towel with a large roll of Sellotape. And when you've been a bit cavalier with the old razor and the sand starts blowing about . . . well, I needn't tell you. . .'

A lot of people had told him that there was a danger that the operation might have a psychological effect on him and that he might . . . not be able to . . . you know . . . whatsit. . .

In the event, his friends' fears proved to be totally unfounded. 'I tried it out within twenty-four hours and it was as great as ever.'

However, as he pointed out, a vasectomee is not immediately sterile and after a month, he is asked to take a sample along to the hospital for testing. In fact, he must do so three times before he can be quite sure that all the stored-up sperm has gone.

'If you can imagine a more gruesome experience than having to slip into the bog at the office and give yourself a quick J. Arthur into this little bottle, I'd like to know of it. It's bad enough having to get in the mood in the first place, but to have to hand over this half a teaspoonful to the nurse who looks at you as if to say, "Is that the best you can do?" well . . .'

All I can say is, anyone who can survive that in their mid-forties, can survive anything.

And that would have been the end of that, as far as I was concerned, had my publisher not been a man with such a tidy mind.

'I wonder,' he said, after reading through the typescript for the first time, 'if the book couldn't do with some concluding comments. A summing up of your thoughts and feelings, if you like. I mean, it does all seem to come to rather an abrupt halt at the end of the sex chapter, and we wouldn't want readers to feel they'd been left hanging in mid-air, as it were.'

I pointed out that actually, I didn't have an awful lot more to say. I had suspected, from the moment I started working on the book, that at forty-three one had scarcely begun to approach the foothills of middle age, and that frankly my qualifications for writing it at all were at least questionable and at worst downright dishonest. Now, after countless conversations on the subject with men and women of all ages and walks of life, several months of considered thought, and some eighty thousand words, I was convinced of it.

All right, so I had more or less covered the ground, made a few sympathetic noises, scratched some familiar itches, even told people things they may not have known before. But for all that, only a man who had been through middle age and out the other end should dare to tell others how to survive it. I had gaily announced that middle age ran from forty to sixty, and yet generally speaking, apart from the odd unaccountable twinge here and there (mostly there), and the occasional moment of panic at the gathering speed with which life suddenly seemed to be hurtling by, I had never felt in better form in my life. But then, of course, for some of us, middle age is always something that's going to happen next year.

'Fine', he said, 'Why don't you say that then?'

'Fine,' I said.

So I have.